UNIVERSITY OF NORTH CAROLINA AT CHAPEL HILL

DEPARTMENT OF ROMANCE LANGUAGES

NORTH CAROLINA STUDIES
IN THE ROMANCE LANGUAGES AND LITERATURES

ESSAYS; TEXTS, TEXTUAL STUDIES AND TRANSLATIONS; SYMPOSIA

Founder: URBAN TIGNER HOLMES

D1103771

Distributed by:

UNIVERSITY OF NORTH CAROLINA PRESS

CHAPEL HILL
North Carolina 27514
U.S.A.

NORTH CAROLINA STUDIES IN THE
ROMANCE LANGUAGES AND LITERATURES

Essays 13

THE THEATER OF ARTHUR ADAMOV

THE THEATER OF ARTHUR ADAMOV

BY

JOHN J. McCANN

CHAPEL HILL

NORTH CAROLINA STUDIES IN THE ROMANCE
LANGUAGES AND LITERATURES
U.N.C. DEPARTMENT OF ROMANCE LANGUAGES
1975

Library of Congress Cataloging in Publication Data

McCann, John Joseph.
    The theater of Arthur Adamov.

    (North Carolina Studies in the Romance Languages and Literatures: Essays; 13)
    Bibliography: p.
    Includes index.
    1. Adamov, Arthur—Criticism and interpretation.

I. Title. II. Series.

PQ2601.D323Z77   842'.9'14   75-29323
ISBN 0-88438-013-0

I.S.B.N. 0-88438-013-0

IMPRESO EN ESPAÑA

PRINTED IN SPAIN

DEPÓSITO LEGAL: V. 3.758 - 1975

ARTES GRÁFICAS SOLER, S. A. - JÁVEA, 28 - VALENCIA (8) - 1975

To A. A. with gratitude

ACKNOWLEDGMENTS

I should like to express my gratitude to Professor Carlos Lynes of the University of Pennsylvania who inspired and guided my work from beginning to end. I am also deeply grateful to Professors Bernhardt Blumenthal and Richard Boudreau of La Salle College for the time and energy they devoted to the final stages of the manuscript.

I should like to acknowledge my indebtedness to La Salle College for its generosity in awarding me a grant which made possible the completion of my work.

A special word of appreciation is due Don H. who said, "Isn't it about time you finished that thing?"

jjmc

CONTENTS

INTRODUCTION

Arthur Adamov (1908-1970), first recognized in the 1950's as one of the triumvirate of the then developing "theater of the absurd" — Beckett, Ionesco, and Adamov — and later established as a major voice in the politically oriented "left wing" theater of the 1960's, created a body of work which reflects most of the major tendencies of the French theater of his time. Perhaps no other contemporary playwright better synthesizes the diverse orientations of the French theater during this extremely rich period.

Of the twenty original plays written between 1947 and 1970, at least three have been selected for anthologies designed to introduce the reader to the French avant-garde theater. Yet this same author had become by the mid 1960's the major spokesman for the politically committed theater of France. This apparent contradiction in orientation and design has been Adamov's original and significant contribution to modern French theater. His work represents the slow and sometimes painful elaboration of a synthesis without parallel in the twentieth century. As the French critic and friend of the playwright Marc Rombaut points out in an article written at the time of Adamov's death, the reconciliation of designs was both difficult and original.

> Placé sous le signe de la névrose obsessionnelle et de l'engagement politique, le théâtre d'Adamov tente alors une réconciliation difficile, originale. [1]

And yet at the same time this apparent dichotomy in Adamov's work leads to at least a partial explanation of a career whose promise

---

[1] Marc Rombaut, "Arthur Adamov 1908-1970," *French Review* (October, 1971), p. 6.

was never satisfactorily fulfilled. Success eluded him as both the public and the critics misjudged his work, forcing it to fit pre-established categories that have little to do with his reconciliation of divergent designs. Thus while Beckett had received a Nobel Prize and Ionesco had entered the *Académie française*, Adamov failed to achieve the stature and esteem he so desperately sought. By 1967 he considered abandoning the theater, blaming his bad health on the failure of the critics to appreciate the significance of his efforts.

> Le théâtre aussi. L'abandonner? Je me sentais vraiment trop biffé, exclu, proscrit. J'ai déjà dit que ma maladie était en partie imputable à mes déceptions professionnelles. [2]

Dead by suicide in 1970, Adamov leaves behind a huge body of work which has not had the success it deserves, but which remains among the most remarkable of our times by virtue of its honesty, purity and unity.

Arthur Adamov was born of wealthy Armenian parents on the 23rd. of August, 1908, in Kislovodsk in the Caucasus. Like the children of many well-to-do Russian families of the time, Adamov was brought up in French and has always considered it his native language. Forced to leave Russia when Arthur was only four years old because of the ominous political situation, the family was at Freudenstadt in the Black Forest when the First World War broke out. Persecuted as citizens of an enemy nation, the Adamovs fled Germany and took refuge in Geneva where with the help of the famous theatrical family, the Pitoëffs, young Arthur attended the Rosset school.

With the triumph of the Bolshevik revolution in 1918 and the subsequent nationalization of the Adamov oil fields near Kislovodsk, the family suddenly went from very rich to very poor, a traumatic experience that was to have serious repercussions on Adamov and his work. When the war ended, the family returned to Germany and settled for a few years in Mainz where Arthur studied at the French *lycée*. It was here, as Adamov was to intimate later in his plays, that his father spent increasingly greater amounts of time gambling at the Casino in an effort to recoup the family's financial losses.

---

[2] Arthur Adamov, *L'Homme et l'enfant* (Paris, 1968), p. 232.

In 1924, when Adamov was sixteen years old, the family settled in Paris where the playwright completed his studies at the Lycée Lakanal, at Bourg-la-Reine. Except for short sojourns in Ireland, Italy, Yugoslavia, Cuba, Portugal, the United States and especially Germany, Paris remained the geographical center of his activities until the day he died. He was quickly absorbed into Parisian bohemia, frequenting especially Surrealist circles and becoming a curious but familiar figure of Left Bank cafés. From 1927 on he devoted himself almost exclusively to literary life and politics, a combination which was to shape the dual thrusts of his theater. During this period he edited *Discontinuité*, an avant-garde periodical, and wrote poetry of a Surrealist nature. His friends included Eluard, Artaud, Cocteau, Blin as well as Giacometti and Modigliani.

After his father's death by suicide in 1933, Adamov gradually stopped writing and experienced the first of what would be a long series of spiritual, psychological and ultimately physical crises. His return to active literary life began in 1938 with the recording and analysis of his first descent into hell. Finished in 1943 and published in 1946, *L'Aveu* is a short, powerful and ruthlessly honest prose document of confession and self-revelation, an act of exorcism by autobiography which in effect freed Adamov for the theater. It documents the years of the war, his internment in the concentration camp of Argelès in 1941, his sado-masochism, endless sufferings and humiliations, his fears and obsessions and finally his need to persist in spite of the complete absence of illusions and facile solutions.

In the years immediately following the war and prior to the writing of his first play in 1947, Adamov dedicated himself to the short-lived literary review *L'Heure nouvelle*, of which he was the editor and for which, along with René Char, Antonin Artaud, Marthe Robert and Roger Gilbert-Lecomte, he wrote numerous short articles. In the social and political spheres Adamov had by this time worked out a personally plausible adhesion to Communism as the least damaging of systems. Thus in a certain sense he was prepared psychologically to devote himself to the writing of theater, a need that he had admitted to himself and others ever since his first reading of Strindberg in the 1940's.

Adamov wrote *La Parodie,* his first major play, in 1947. *L'Invasion* followed in 1949. But it wasn't until 1950 and his third play, *La grande et la petite manœuvre,* that an Adamov play was first produced on the 11th. of November at the Théâtre des Noctambules in Paris under the direction of Jean-Marie Serreau. Three days later Jean Vilar produced *L'Invasion* at the Studio des Champs-Elysées. And finally in June of 1952 his first play *La Parodie* was performed at the Théâtre de Lancry under the direction of Rober Blin. Yet by 1953 Adamov had written some seven plays and was regarded by many as potentially the most significant new figure to appear in the French theater since the war.

Adamov enjoyed the professional success of those early years. For the first time in his life he felt part of something, the Beckett-Ionesco-Adamov trio that dominated the new *anti-théâtre* of the 1950's. It was, however, to be a short lived joy, for by 1955 the three playwrights had already begun to move in different directions. *Le Ping-Pong* marked for most audiences and critics the beginning of a new orientation in the theater of Adamov. With *Paolo Paoli* in 1956 he seemed to move further in the direction of Brechtian epic theater. By *Le Printemps* 71 of 1961 Adamov was no longer considered part of the new avant-garde and his plays were drawing strongly unfavorable reactions from former admirers who critized the "didactic" and "discursive" elements in his new work. Adamov had entered into a long dry period of semi-failures.

He continued to write throughout the 1960's saddened by the loss of a sense of belonging, bitter at the public's failure to comprehend the thrust of his work, and more and more subject to physical, mental and spiritual deterioration. In 1965 he suffered a pulmonary congestion. In 1966 he was admitted to the clinic at Épiney for alcoholism. After his release he experienced loss of memory, hallucinations and problems of sight which led to psychiatric treatment at the clinic of La Pitié. In 1967 he contracted tuberculosis (his mother had died of T.B. in 1942) and went to Switzerland for treatment. More and more he relied on alcohol and other drugs to sustain his miserable existence. But as he tells us in the autobiographical *L'Homme et l'enfant* of 1968, he suffered most of all from a feeling of seprateness, of being between parentheses, in the margins of his time and its theater. On the 15th. of March 1970, alone in his own apartment on the Rue Champollion in Paris, Arthur "Ern" Adamov committed suicide at the age of sixty-one.

No biographical sketch of Adamov's life, no matter how detailed, can capture with justice the intensity of suffering, the degradation, humiliation and finally the triumph and purity of so complex and haunted a man. The significant and determining factors in his life and work — his family's sudden loss of wealth, his father's gambling and suicide, the internment at the prison camp of Argelès, his own obsessions, neuroses and alcoholism and finally the ignominy of his professional failure — are the dominating themes so vividly evoked in the autobiographical prose works *L'Aveu*, *L'Homme et l'enfant* and *Je....ils*. From the opening cry of *L'Aveu* in 1938,

> Ce qu'il y a? Je sais d'abord qu'il y a moi. Mais qui est moi? Mais qu'est-ce que moi? Tout ce que je sais de moi, c'est que je souffre. Et si je souffre c'est qu'à l'origine de moi-même il y a mutilation, séparation. Je suis séparé. Ce dont je suis séparé, je ne sais pas le nommer. Mais je suis séparé. Autrefois, cela s'appelait Dieu. Maintenant, il n'y a plus de nom. [3]

to the humiliating admission of *L'Homme et l'enfant* in 1965,

> Importance d'obtenir la victoire sur le plan professionnel. Se sentir affirmé, pousser en avant. Ne plus être le commis voyageur, le pauvre type qui gagne dans ses tournées quelques livres ou quelques westmarks. Triompher dans son propre travail et son propre pays, le pays dans la langue duquel on écrit. [4]

we can follow in agonizing detail the honest and lucid account of a major playwright's struggle, triumph and failure.

But in the final analysis it is the plays themselves which tell us more about the man. From the endless humiliations of his early protagonists to the disabling alcoholism of M. le Modéré in the play of the same name, we see repeated exorcisms of the evil spirits that haunted the playwright. Inevitably in the final two plays, *Off Limits* and *Si l'été revenait,* suicide appears as a viable alternative to despair, defeat and disillusionment. It is the end of a sad tale expertly told by a master craftsman.

The theater of Adamov reflects his European as well as his French background. While the principal influences on his work are French —

---

[3] Arthur Adamov, *L'Aveu* (Paris, 1946), p. 19.
[4] Arthur Adamov, *L'Homme et l'enfant* (Paris, 1968), p. 174.

Jarry, Apollinaire, Surrealism and Artaud — Adamov's theater assimilates much that is primarily of German-Russian origin — Büchner, Strindberg, Gogol, Chekov, Gorky, Kafka, German Expressionism and Brecht. This combination of influences leads in Adamov to a wholly "un-French" theater, a non-verbal, pre-rational "literal" theater of protest that stands as the antithesis of both Classical French drama and the traditional well-made play of the 19th. and 20th. centuries.

It is the theater of Alfred Jarry which is the seminal French influence on Adamov and the whole modern avant-garde theater. But it is Jarry's work as experienced, refined and amplified by Apollinaire and Artaud that ultimately shapes Adamov's theater. Jarry's revolt against bourgeois mentality and traditional forms leads in Adamov to dramatic structures which reflect on the formal level the chaotic, anarchic revolt of the play's substance. Adamov's "scream of protest" hurled against the absurdity of the human condition and the degradation of its man-made socio-political systems is, as G. E. Wellwarth points out in an article on Jarry, indeed inherited from the creator of Père Ubu.

> The fact that Jarry's mind remained in many essentials that of a child in no way diminishes his importance as the originator of the scream of protest which Antonin Artaud later decreed as the official theme of the avant-garde drama. [5]

It is especially the early plays of Adamov which reflect the influence of Jarry. For in their primitiveness, their subjectivist and expressionistic approach, in their stories freed of time and place and lacking verisimilitude, we see reflections of Jarry's attempt to tear down the veil of habit separating us from the real, to deny the "reality" of time, space and man by deliberate anachronisms, confusion and "puppet-like" characters who speak in monotone an automatic and rudimentary language.

This disorienting element in Jarry's theater is elevated by Apollinaire in his essay "L'Esprit nouveau et les poètes" to the status of a principle. For in Apollinaire's notion of the "modern" the principle of surprise is the touchstone. It is the necessary element needed to shock the spectator. The investigation of form that Apollinaire so

---

[5] G. E. Wellwarth, "Alfred Jarry: the seed of the avant-garde drama," *Criticism*, IV (1962), pp. 109-110.

strongly advocates, the "new realism" that he prophesies, and the autonomous universe of the play evoked in the preface to *Les Mamelles de Tirésias* are contributing factors to the shocking and scandalous experience which is Adamov's theater. It is a universe where the unexpected and improbable appear eminently possible, logical and even at times inevitable.

And yet the single most direct influence on Adamov, especially in the early plays, is his exposure to the doctrines and experiments of Surrealism and Artaud. Adamov's use of the theater to exorcise neurosis and exploit dream stems directly from Surrealist faith in the redemptive value of man's subconscious mind. His creation on stage of an unpredictable world is a concrete and dramatic incarnation of the Surrealist experiment which, by changing our angle of perception and abandoning traditional time-place sequences, forces us to experience directly the relativity of our ideas and our conception of reality.

Of all the avant-garde playwrights of the last twenty-five years it is perhaps Adamov who most faithfully incorporates into his plays the theory and experiments of his friend and teacher Antonin Artaud. For the theater of Adamov is above all else a "metaphysical" theater, a theater which literally and concretely demonstrates man's perilous position in a universe whose sky might very well fall in. It is a shattering theater, disturbing and disorienting which, faithful to Artaud's notion of the theater of cruelty, dramatizes violence, perversion, crime, derangement, repression and sadism as means to awaken in its audience a new consciousness of human potentiality beyond the limited role fossilized civilization affords it. It does not discuss man's predicament in philosophical terms. It does not explain man's dilemma in psychological language. Rather it reveals in concrete images filling the physical space of the stage the precariousness of human existence, and by so doing reflects Artaud's *Le Théâtre et son double*.

> Il ne s'agit pas d'assassiner le public avec des préoccupations cosmiques transcendantes. Qu'il ait des clefs profondes de la pensée et de l'action selon lesquelles lire tout le spectacle, cela ne regarde pas en général le spectateur, qui ne s'y intéresse pas. Mais encore faut-il qu'elles y soient; et cela nous regarde. [6]

---

[6] Antonin Artaud, *Le Théâtre et son double* (Paris, 1964), p. 141.

Consistent with Artaudian principles, Adamov creates a theatrical universe which questions fundamental, accepted values while at the same time spoofing the pretentions and comfortable self-satisfactions of rationalism. It rejects the dogmas of naturalism and responds to Artaud's demand for a return to myth and magic, for a new language of theater, a spatial language whereby the audience would experience directly in the play's concrete and literal orchestration of space, rhythm, gesture, pattern and sign the surreality of man's existence. Thus Adamov's notion of "le sens littéral" responds directly to Artaud's plea for a new "métaphysique de la parole, du geste, de l'expression."

> Il s'agit donc, pour le théâtre, de créer une métaphysique de la parole, du geste, de l'expression, en vue de l'arracher à son piétinement psychologique et humain. Mais tout ceci ne peut servir s'il n'y a derrière un tel effort une sorte de tentation métaphysique réelle, un appel à certaines idées inhabituelles, dont le destin est justement de ne pouvoir être limitées, ni même formellement dessinées. Ces idées qui touchent à la Création, au Devenir, au Chaos, et sont toutes d'ordre cosmique, fournissent une première notion d'un domaine dont le théâtre s'est totalement déshabitué. Elles peuvent créer une sorte d'équation passionnante entre l'Homme, la Société, la Nature et les Objects. [7]

But the theater of Arthur Adamov is European as well as French. He admired such diverse authors as Chekov, Rilke, Kafka and O'Casey. He translated or adapted for the stage works by Büchner, Gorky and Gogol. The strongest foreign or non-French influences reflected in his own work derive from Büchner, Strindberg, German Expressionism and Brecht. An it is in this sense that the theater of Adamov is in part the product of a basically Germanic tradition of playwrights who sought among other things to give concrete expression to the notion of theater as an autonomous art inseparable from the physical space of the stage.

Georg Büchner (1813-1837), whose play *Dantons Tod* Adamov translated for Jean Vilar and the *Festival d'Avignon* of 1948, can in retrospect be seen as the fountainhead of an attitude, perpetuated by Strindberg, German Expressionism, Artaud, Brecht and the Theater

---

[7] Antonin Artaud, *Le Théâtre et son double* (Paris, 1964), pp. 136-137.

of the Absurd, which views the play as a means to disorient its spectators and shatter their illusions. Adamov's own theater reflects especially the dual preoccupation of Büchner with the individual as well as society and its political systems. *Woyzeck* is a brutal drama whose hero, much like the protagonists of Adamov's theater, is both tortured by his own obsessions and nightmares and persecuted by the selfishness and cruelty of others. Moreover, Büchner's concept of politics in the theater as seen in *Dantons Tod* anticipates Adamov's treatment of the political dimension as not bounded by "politics," but rather as an intimation of the larger historical and even existential dimensions of the universe.

Adamov credits Auguste Strindberg (1849-1912) with being the playwright who first attracted him to the theater.

> Car je crois bien que c'est Strindberg, ou plus exactement
> *Le Songe,* qui m'a invité à écrire pour le théâtre. [8]

For Strindberg was the first to dramatize successfully the dreams and obsessions which haunted him, the first to concretize in theatrical dimensions the subjective reality of his inner states of consciousness. Strindberg's use of the logical but ultimately incoherent form of the dream becomes for Adamov, especially in his early plays, a vehicle of exorcism, a means whereby those obsessions which made him suffer most triumph in their most literal expression.

Adamov's excellent study of Strindberg and his theater, *Auguste Strindberg, Dramaturge,* reveals numerous other parallels, both thematic and formal, between the Swedish and French playwrights. Not only is the book a thorough investigation of Strindbergian dramaturgy, but it demonstrates that the origins of both German Expressionism and Adamov's "literal" theater lie in Strindberg's earlier experiments.

> Les paroles des personnages de Strindberg sont imprégnées
> de ce sens littéral sans lequel il n'est pas de théâtre. [9]

Adamov recognized Strindberg as the first playwright to question the efficacy of traditional dialogue, to abandon the habitual word play of

---

[8] Arthur Adamov, *Auguste Strindberg, Dramaturge* (Paris, 1955), p. 8.
[9] Arthur Adamov, *Auguste Strindberg, Dramaturge* (Paris, 1955), p. 69.

questions and answers, and to substitute a "discontinuous" dialogue which would better reflect the reality of a life where no one truly hears another. From Strindberg he also learned the value of variation, how to enrich the monotony of his obsessions by numberless variations and semi-repetitions. Moreover, Adamov never totally escaped the powerful enchantment of the Swedish master. While Strindberg's influence is more obvious in Adamov's early plays, it is persistent throughout all of his theater and becomes in the final stage of Adamov's career even more pronounced.

Like the young Bertolt Brecht, Adamov was deeply impressed by the experiments of German Expressionism. The small circle of poets, playwrights and prose writers of 1910-1920 in Germany introduced or developed many of the modern themes and techniques that were to bear fruit in the French avant-garde theater of the 1950's. And while the plays of Yvan Goll, Ernst Barlach, Georg Kaiser and Ernst Toller go relatively unnoticed today, their influence is especially apparent in the theaters of Ionesco and Adamov. Central to Expressionist theater was the notion of the internal collapse of modern man, his loss of a unifying spiritual center or core. In both Expressionist theater and in the plays of Adamov this collapse or disintegration of personality is visually dramatized on stage by the discontinuity of man's action, a result of the playwright's deliberate rejection of motivation as a factor in man's behavior. In both theaters language, traditional language, has failed, and to solve man's problem of communication, a new and visual language is shaped wherein objects are used to express inner realities or to objectify those thoughts and feelings beyond ordinary language. Like Expressionist drama, Adamov's theater turns away from the banal complexities of traditional psychological theater toward a primitivism wherein parody and political preoccupations mingle freely with his description of a tormented inner hell.

Adamov alternately condemned and praised Bertolt Brecht (1899-1956). He was consistently aware of Brecht's theater from it earliest beginnings in Expressionism to its later fulfillment in the socially committed epic theater with which Brecht is usually associated. But it is only during the central period of Adamov's work (1956-1966), when the emphasis shifts from man as an alienated existential being to man as a dominated and degraded socio-political unit, that Adamov's theater bears witness to Brechtian influence. In these "political" plays, Adamov, like Brecht, demonstrates the immediate responsibility of man to correct political and social injustices. For while ultimately, according to Adamov, these corrupt systems have their roots in the fabric of the human condition, they are nevertheless within the power of man to correct, and therefore the theater can and must enter into history. To fulfill the playwright's responsibility to make man aware of man and his degradation of man Adamov learned from Brecht the need to distance his audience so that they remain "critical," free to judge the causes and remedies of the anguish portrayed on stage. The political options intimated in Adamov's plays as well as the epic structures characteristic of this period in Adamov's development parallel the German playwright's later work. And yet, like Brecht, Adamov continued to use many of the same avant-garde "expressionistic" techniques developed in his earlier plays.

But finally, and perhaps more important than any literary influence, is Adamov's own experience of life itself. What he saw, what he heard and the difference between the two is, in his own words, the point of departure towards one of the richest, most unified and unique theaters of the recent past.

> J'au vu tous les lieux où les hommes se rencontrent sans se voir, se côtoient sans se toucher, se touchent sans se comprendre, et c'est cela qui m'a donné une image vivante de la scène. En se rencontrant sans se voir, on se parle pourtant, et c'est le sentiment de cette étrange résistance du language qui m'a donné envie d'écrire des dialogues. [10]

In the chapters that follow we intend to study the development and apparent reorientation of Adamov's theater, its seemingly contradictory designs, its ultimate unity and its role in helping to define the contemporary avant-garde and political theaters of France. Our procedure will be to examine each of the twenty plays separately in an effort to discover its basic structure, thematic statement, and unifying factor. The plays are then studied comparatively as variants of each other rather than as departures from a fixed model or prototype as established by any one play. They are then grouped into units which are determined principally by the emphases which the plays themselves place on particular aspects of Adamov's world vision and evolving dramaturgy. These categories or units are further studied as

---

[10] Arthur Adamov, "La Parodie," *Arts* (29 mai au 4 juin, 1952), p. 13.

variants of each other in an attempt to determine the unifying or consistent factor within the theater of Adamov.

While varied in texture and emphasis the five groups are unified on a formal level by a repetitive structure of intensification as well as by the consistent presence of clearly avant-garde techniques even in the more "realistic" plays. On a thematic plane Adamov's entire work from *La Parodie* to *Si l'été revenait* depicts and criticizes a world characterized by absence, absence of *a priori* values, absence of communication, absence of dignity, and finally absence of man's awareness of and concern for his fellow man.

CHAPTER I

THE INTERIOR-HELL PLAYS

It is the dual character of man's predicament before the void of existence that permeates the theater of Adamov, both man's historical situation and his natural state. Man stands alone, incapable of communicating, defenseless, deprived before God and State. He is a prisoner of the State, condemned to annihilation in death or subservience to the inescapable, destructive human condition. As the accent shifts in varying degrees within the work from the historical and more apparently remediable suffering of man to the seemingly inescapable anguish of the natural law, it becomes more and more apparent that the two levels of damnation are intimately interwoven.

The interior drama (drama within) of Adamov's characters is closely paralleled by the exterior drama (drama without) of their specific conditions. The human condition (the interior hell) is paralleled by the social conditions (the exterior hell) of man's fate. The two in effect are manifestations of the same malaise, the same void or absence, and while the more existential conflict remains insoluble, the politico-social conflict is seen at various stages of his theater to be less or more resolvable. This accounts for the various shifts from stark pessimism to faint hope, from evidently apolitical situations to political resolutions in the latter plays.

Adamov's theater is the statement of life lived with the full realization of the absence of what we might call the spiritual dimension.

> Mais qui est moi? Mais qu'est-ce que moi? Tout ce que je sais de moi, c'est que je souffre. Et si je souffre c'est qu'à l'origine de moi-même il y a mutilation, séparation. Je suis séparé. Ce dont je suis séparé, je ne sais par le nommer.

Mais je suis séparé. Autrefois, cela s'appelait Dieu. Maintenant, il n'y a plus de nom. [1]

Adamov's theater emphasizes an interior conflict, a war within self that parallels the external conflicts of man against man. Moreover, Adamov's theater is not an explanation of man's condition — there are no answers that man is capable of finding — but an intensely felt evocation of man's anguish, an anguish more sharply felt, intensified by his vague awareness of the lost spiritual realm. His blindness is not congenital. The "weight of total guilt, the nameless fears, the vain longings for lucid order and pure love" [2] are symptoms of the void that the theater of Adamov depicts so concretely and seeks to fill. For filling the physical space of the stage is for Adamov an act of revolt, the act of man seeking to fill the void within.

Of the eight plays written between 1947 and 1953, four plays stand out as the most explicit yet abstract statement of man's existence as an absence, as a void to be filled, as a lost spiritual dimension. These four plays are at one of the extreme limits of the work's basic statement; the most apolitical, asocial and therefore existential statement of man's dilemma. In these plays the drama is free to unfold against the relatively neutral backdrop of timelessness and spacelessness. We are nowhere and everywhere, at no time and at any time, totally freed of place, time and known characters. Its protagonists are almost solely preoccupied by the intimate dilemma of reintegration and harmony, of reconciliation. They are static dramas with little in the way of conventional plot and psychological motivation. Rather the theater of Adamov is man's fate — his solitude, his lack of communication, his inexplicable fears, remorse and guilt — concretely, metaphorically and literally situated within a theatrical confine. In his Préface to *Théâtre II* the author recounts his discovery of this "sens littéral," its theatricality, its poetic evocativeness.

Un aveugle demandait l'aumône; deux jeunes filles passèrent près de lui sans le voir, le bousculèrent par mégarde; elles chantaient: "J'ai fermé les yeux, c'était merveilleux..." L'idée me vint alors de montrer sur la scène, le plus grossièrement et le plus visiblement possible, la solitude humaine,

[1] Arthur Adamov, *L'Aveu* (Paris, 1946), p. 19.
[2] Carlos Lynes, Jr., "Adamov or 'Le sens littéral' in the theater," *Yale French Studies*, No. 14 (Winter 1954-55), p. 55.

> l'absence de communication. Autrement dit, d'un phénomène
> vrai entre d'autres, je tirais une "métaphysique." Après trois
> ans de travail, et de multiples versions — dont la première
> mettait en scène l'aveugle lui-même! — ce fut *La Parodie*.[3]

Man's fate is depicted literally and intensified by repetition until it
reaches a tragic pitch. This is the prevailing tension structure of the
entire *œuvre,* wherein man's psychological states are objectified on
stage, their representation increasing in power by virtue of ceaseless
repetition.

The texture of each play, the independent character of the detail,
varies slightly, more apparently from grouping to grouping, but the
repetitive structure of intensification so indicative of the early plays
prevails throughout all of his work. The invariant or structure of the
plays is then a progression towards a gradual, then rapid disintegration of the play's universe. The disintegration itself results from the
intensification of the prevailing, always present "absence," an absence
whose concretization varies from play to play — woman's love, political cause, redeeming message, identity, etc. Of the four "interior-
hell" plays this absence intensified is perhaps best felt in *L'Invasion.*

The play's plot is apparently the story of Pierre, his wife Agnès,
his friend Tradel and his mother seeking within the confines of one
room to unravel the mystery of the manuscript left in fragments by
the dead friend Jean. The project is, of course, a failure during which
Pierre is ostensibly betrayed by his wife who takes a lover, le Premier
Venu, as well as by his friend who betrays him to the authorities.
Pierre finally abandons the quest, seeks solace in his wife, discovers
her gone, and apparently commits suicide. But the plot line of an
Adamov play is little more than a musical score.

> It would be vain to outline the "plot" of an Adamov play
> or analyze the "psychology" of the characters, for these
> terms — at least in their conventional meanings — simply do
> not apply to the "univers créé" which Adamov brings to the
> theater.[4]

Writing in a truly "modern" vein, influenced by the "new aes-
thetics," Surrealism and German Expressionism, Adamov's theater

[3] Arthur Adamov, *Note préliminaire* in *Théâtre II* (Paris, 1955), p. 8.
[4] Lynes, p. 56.

uses evident reality as a sculptor uses clay, to be shaped, molded, transformed thereby producing a truer, inner, less evident reality. It is a theater which responds to Apollinaire's definition in *Les Mamelles de Tirésias* of a play as a complete and created universe.

> Son univers est sa pièce
> A l'intérieur de laquelle il est le dieu créateur
> Qui dispose à son gré
> Les sons les gestes les démarches les masses les couleurs
> Non pas dans le seul but
> De photographier ce qu'on appelle une tranche de vie
> Mais pour faire surgir la vie même dans toute sa vérité
> Car la pièce doit être un univers complet
> Avec son créateur
> C'est-à-dire la nature même
> Et non pas seulement
> La représentation d'un petit morceau
> De ce qui nous entoure ou de ce qui s'est jadis passé [5]

It is also a theater which demands production, a non-literary theater in the sense that the written text is but one of the parts helping to fill the physical space of the stage. The presence of meaning within an Adamov play is posited not only by the text but also by the physical presence of objects and characters, their absence and juxtaposition. This need for concretization in production makes itself felt as one imaginatively follows the text.

> Je veux dire que, lisant, je me sentais contraint à devenir metteur en scène. Puis acteur. Enfin actrice. [6]

This type of predominantly non-verbal theater with its stress on the physical, on the literal, sustains, reflects and advances the world vision posited in the works of Adamov. It coincides with the structure of intensification that dominates the playwright's entire canon. The play begins with a statement of absence, apparently the absence of

---

[5] Guillaume Apollinaire, *Les Mamelles de Tirésias* (Paris, 1946), pp. 31-32.

[6] Jacques Lemarchand in Arthur Adamov, *La Parodie, L'Invasion,* précédées d'une lettre d'André Gide, et des témoignages de René Char, Jacques Prévert, Henri Thomas, Jacques Lemarchand, Jean Vilar, Roger Blin (Paris, 1950), p. 15.

meaning which the manuscript promises but so far has failed to deliver.

> The most oppressive presence is an absence. [7]

> A play about the hopeless search for meaning, the quest for a message that will make sense in a jumble of undecipherable papers: but it is concerned with order and disorder in society as well as in the family. [8]

The disintegration of the play's universe results from the gradual disintegration of the quest for meaning within the manuscript and is literally depicted in the disintegration of the unit Pierre-Agnès-Tradel. The absence of meaning posited in Act I is attenuated by the quest itself and the union of the three symbolized by the "tu" of their dialogue. But by Act II Agnès has refused to work any longer for the perfectionist Pierre who in turn has more and more trouble communicating with Tradel.

> Ne m'en veuillez pas, mais depuis quelque temps, je ne peux plus tutoyer personne. [9]

The message continues to elude Pierre. There is a growing absence of communication.

> On ne voit plus clair. [10]

By Act III the "vous" is displaced by silence, Pierre retires into a nook of the room, the message of the manuscript has become "plat."

> tout ce que j'ai tiré de l'ombre ordonné, retrouvé, reste désespérément sans relief ... Je ne chercherai plus rien. (Pause.) J'attendrai dans le silence, immobile. [11]

And as he abandons the quest, the absence is intensified and objectified by the flight of his wife, who leaves him at the end of the act,

[7] Lynes, p. 51.
[8] Martin Esslin, *The Theatre of the Absurd* (New York, 1961), p. 55.
[9] Arthur Adamov, *L'Invasion* in *Théâtre I* (Paris, 1953), p. 76.
[10] *L'Invasion*, p. 77.
[11] *L'Invasion*, p. 86.

for as she says to her new lover, "Non, tout est dit." [12] There is no longer anything to be said. There is only an absence of communication.

When in Act IV Pierre emerges from his retreat, it is to announce the abandonment of his quest, to destroy the manuscript while proclaiming that he now accepts life without meaning.

> Je suis bien décidé à vivre comme tout le monde. Ce que j'ai compris là, c'est que rien ne me sera donné tant que je n'aurai pas trouvé le moyen de mener une vie tout à fait ordinaire. [13]

Total absence freely accepted, the revolt abandoned, is then concretized for him by the absence of his wife, the betrayal by Tradel. He leaves the room, which is now physically and spiritually dominated by the castrating mother, and completes the disintegration by total absence in death.

Paralleling the disintegration of the play's universe and part of the very process is the corresponding "invasion" of the title. As the spiritual dimension hinted at in the indecipherable manuscript fades and becomes more elusive, the invasion of things and people becomes more pronounced. The absence of value is thus made more and more oppressive by the growing invasion or encroachment by venial matter. The void must be filled and if not spiritually, then physically.

But there is, of course, the invasion of man's existence by meaning. The manuscript promises a redemptive message. This, in the play's terms, is the only major positive invasion.

> Et c'est là le sujet secret de ce drame: cette active présence posthume, puis après des tentatives de survie, son progressif puis définitif anéantissement. [14]

The "tentatives de survie" are physically pictured by the growing encumbrance of the stage in Acts I and II, while Pierre is still searching, before the silence and death of Acts III and IV. The apparent physical order of the room with papers neatly arranged of Act III indicates to us the beginning of renunciation and the total domination

---

[12] *L'Invasion,* p. 87.
[13] *L'Invasion,* p. 92.
[14] André Gide in Arthur Adamov, *La Parodie, L'Invasion,* p. 10.

of the castrating mother-figure. By Act IV, when Pierre announces his abandonment of the quest, when Agnès has gone to her lover, when Tradel has betrayed his friend, apparent order and comfort reign, and the mother's chair now occupies stage center.

In close parallel to this inner drama is the geopolitical invasion feared by the mother and her friend. She battles to preserve her country from the unknown as she seeks to protect and dominate her son. The frontiers must be closed. This uncertain dilemma is resolved by Act IV when the immigration has been stopped and there is apparent order and stability. Once again absence has been intensified.

We see here an example of the intertwining of personal and socio-political dramas so prevalent in the theater of Adamov. Even in this most abstract "interior-hell" play there is reference to social considerations just as we shall later see in the more overtly "political" and "social" plays. This particular theme of man's rejection of "les autres" can be traced in increasing proportions from grouping to grouping, most noticeably in *Tous contre tous* of the "police-state" plays and *La Politique des restes* of the "social" plays.

Perhaps the most obvious manifestation of the invasion of disorder within the play's world is the arrival of Le Premier Venu and his seduction of Agnès. Agnès, Jean's sister and Pierre's wife, was along with Pierre the one most capable of deciphering the manuscript's message. It is she who can best aid Pierre in the search for order and meaning. She is, therefore, the mother's arch rival and her influence must be and is destroyed. In Act I she works along with her husband. In Act II she is no longer part of the unit seeking to decipher the message. In Act III she debates whether to leave with Le Premier Venu. As she is increasingly rejected, she turns more and more to the one who offers her praise and comfort, and it is only at the very end of the act that she finally leaves.

> La lumière revient. Lumière crue. On voit le Premier Venu, Agnès dans les bras, se diriger vers la porte de droite. Agnès tient un imperméable qu'elle laisse traîner sur le sol. Le Premier Venu est chargé de deux manteaux. La Mère éclate d'un rire grossier en se tapant sur les cuisses. [15]

---

[15] *L'Invasion*, p. 89.

The resolution of a complex drama — man's reliance on the redeeming female, her role as soul-mate in the quest for meaning, her
failure to permanently fill the void of longing — is thus literally portrayed in these most banal of terms. This too, in the world of Adamov's theater, is part of the human condition, part of the endless
humiliation to which we are subjected.

> Pourquoi toujours cette médiocrité de la vie qui rapetisse
> tout? Pourquoi un drame intérieur se résoud-il presque tou-
> jours en un acte symbolique dégradant? [16]

Pierre's quest for order and meaning in life, for what we have called
the spiritual dimension, is continually thwarted. He can discover no
way out of the human predicament. While totally devoting himself
to the manuscript, he loses his wife and friend. By abandoning the
manuscript to lead what he calls an ordinary life with wife and
friends, etc., he has lost or betrayed their point of union, their common *raison d'être.* As in the world of *La Parodie,* no matter what
man does, whether he acts or doesn't, he meets frustration and defeat.

> quoiqu'il tente, l'homme se heurte à l'impossible. [17]

The play is then a concrete and literal dramatization of a world
dominated by absence, absence of a redeeming message, of fidelity,
of communication. Man has been castrated by both State and Nature
and stands vulnerable before the human condition. There is a dimension that eludes him.

> il n'est pas donné à l'homme de trouver le chemin qui le
> mène au but. [18]

This loss of the spiritual dimension characterizes the world of Adamov's theater. Its literal manifestations vary from play to play, but
the pronounced absence of this value is what renders the universe of
this and other Adamov plays tragic. In the theater of Adamov man
is radically alone. Adamov himself has defined the "idée maîtresse"

---

[16] *L'Aveu,* p. 138.
[17] *L'Aveu,* p. 9.
[18] *L'Aveu,* p. 10.

of both *La Parodie* and *L'Invasion* as "personne n'entend personne." [19]
But this absence of communication goes even deeper, because the
Adamovian protagonist is also incapable of dialogue within. Pierre cannot fathom the manuscript, Agnès and Tradel cannot fathom Pierre
because all three are prisoners of themselves, incapable of fathoming
the mystery of their existence. While evidently speaking of the manuscript but in reality speaking of himself, Pierre announces to Tradel
and Agnès,

> Ce qu'il me faut, ce n'est pas le sens des mots, c'est leur
> volume et leur corps mouvant. (Pause.) Je ne chercherai plus
> rien. (Pause.) J'attendrai dans le silence, immobile. Je de-
> viendrai très attentif. [20]

It is the "dieu caché" of the tragic world, the dimension that eludes
man, that is at the center of Pierre's condition, what Goldmann calls
the most important character of the tragic universe: fatality, tran-
scendence, God.

> Toujours présent, ce Dieu est en même temps un dieu caché,
> un dieu toujours absent. [21]

The Adamovian hero is tragically alone, a prisoner of the state and
of self. He can alleviate to a certain degree the anguish of his social
condition, but is powerless to satisfy an inner, transcendental longing.
In a world without God, he seeks a spiritual dimension and is incapable of finding "le chemin qui le mène au but." Life is a nightmarish hell punctuated only by the small advances man occasionally
makes in the socio-political sphere. The existential anguish of being
persists, intensified by repetition. There are no remedies.

> il n'y a — j'en suis convaincu maintenant — de remèdes à
> rien sinon à des vétilles. [22]

Thre is only the void of absence, the mysterious, eternally present,
eternally obscure longing that dominates the human condition.

---

[19] *Note préliminaire* in *Théâtre II*, p. 9.
[20] *L'Invasion*, p. 86.
[21] Lucien Goldmann, *Jean Racine, Dramaturge* (Paris, 1956), p. 18.
[22] *L'Aveu*, p. 16.

While later dismissing *L'Invasion* as a "pensum" and a "drame bourgeois," Adamov continued to favor *Le Professeur Taranne* as the most significant of his early plays.

> *Le Professeur Taranne* fut pour moi un événement, car, pour la première fois, je transcrivais simplement un rêve sans chercher à lui conférer un sens général, sans vouloir rien prouver, sans vouloir ajouter à la disculpation vraisembla-blement contenue dans le rêve lui-même, une disculpation intellectuelle. [23]

The play is then the direct rendering on stage of a nightmare and is presented to us with that special logic and order that nightmares have. It is not a psychological study, but rather a faithful recording in dream images in action of the hero's fears, neuroses, and conflicts. It is theater heavily influenced by the theories of Artaud and the work of the earlier Surrealists for whom the domain of the theater was not psychological but plastic, not verbal but physical, not only temporal but spatial, an anti-literary theater relying on modification of earlier non-verbal forms, a "pure theater." [24]

Thus the apparent story of a man arrested for public disrobing on a beach who passes through various scenes of neglect, scorn, mis-recognition and dismissal only to be once again arrested and released for strewing papers on the same beach is also the story of a professor who plagiarized and was found out, the drama of man whose rep-utation, on a social level, and identity, on a metaphysical level, are at stake.

> Like *La Grande et la Petite Manœuvre* this play is the drama of a man's inner dispossession, made manifest by Pro-fessor Taranne's compulsive drive to expose himself phys-ically through morbid fear that others will expose his intel-lectual and moral fraud. [25]

The fear is "morbid," neurotic, and is pictured on the stage by a series of concrete images rather than abstract verbalizations. The identity crisis inherent in the human condition and the fear of expo-

---

[23] *Note préliminaire* in *Théâtre II*, p. 12.
[24] Esslin, p. 238.
[25] Lynes, p. 51.

sure so prevalent in contemporary society are fused and concretized in this drama of a man who, having first been accused of exposing himself and then having been stripped of everything else, exposes himself at the end of the play. For with Taranne the universal question of identity has been intensified by neurosis to the point where it destroys him. He is dramatically interesting exactly because his common defect, as Adamov points out in *L'Aveu*, when pushed to excess becomes exemplary.

> La névrose étant, par nature, grossissement et exagération d'une tare universelle qui existe à l'état embryonnaire en tout être humain, mais dont elle multiplie et renforce les effets, mon mal, de par son caractère propre, devient exemplaire. [26]

What we see on the stage is the literal dispossession of the man — his identity questioned, his veracity impinged, his personality rejected, his fame denied, his whole life threatened. He is left at the end of the play with none of society's defenses. He is stripped of the props of identity, denied the illusion of belonging. He stands naked before his being.

> Having been exposed as a fraud, he exposes himself. It is the nightmare of a man trying to hold on to his identity, unable to establish conclusive proof of it. [27]

The play is a concrete metaphor of man caught in a psychological trap, exposed before others and therefore defeated, humiliated, frightened and abandoned. Taranne is first deprived of his physical freedom by the police, and in the Premier Tableau we see the eventual stripping of all identity and illusion played out against a background where everybody knows everybody else, except him. It is a powerful concretization of the psychological agony of being alone, separated, alienated in the world.

> Du seul fait qu'il existe, l'homme est déjà exilé, expulsé, donc mis hors de tout. [28]

---

[26] *L'Aveu*, p. 11.
[27] Esslin, p. 51.
[28] *L'Aveu*, p. 70

Being mistakenly taken for Professeur Ménard intensifies his loss of identity to the point where he prefers the identity of a Taranne "coupable." This pattern is basically repeated and further intensified by slight variation in the Deuxième Tableau where Taranne is progressively stripped of honor (his post in Belgium), friends and family (his sister), the physical world in which he lives (the décor), and even the illusory notion of honor (the map seating him at the table of honor is empty). There is nothing left. He is revealed as psychologically naked as he physically strips himself of his clothes.

The vision of exile, alienation, and absence of identity posited by the play is shaped by the "farce tragique" form that has been the main genre of the French avant-garde theater of the absurd. As Martin Esslin points out in his *The Theatre of the Absurd*, it is a genre that is both comic and tragic at the same time.

> As the incomprehensibility of the motives, and the often unexplained and mysterious nature of the characters' actions in the Theatre of the Absurd effectively prevent identification, such theatre is a comic theatre in spite of the fact that its subject matter is somber, violent and bitter. [29]

Adamov's dream, *Le Professeur Taranne,* with its refusal to heed the laws of cause and effect, its absence of character motivation, its failure to explain itself verbally and rationally represents a dream-like metaphor of the real universe and of man's fate within it. The "farce tragique" form of this play in which the human condition is represented in concrete poetic images as both comic and deeply tragic is well suited to transmit a vision of the modern world wherein heroism and effective action are absent. The new form responds to the new vision, or as John Crowe Ransom says in *The New Criticism,* it is an act of shaping that experience.

> The creation of a form is nothing more nor less than the act of evaluating and shaping (that is controlling) a given experience. [30]

Once again we are dealing with a theater of absence, man tragically alone in a world deprived of the unknown spiritual dimension that

---

[29] Esslin, p. 301.
[30] John Crowe Ransom, *The New Criticism* (Nowfolk, Conn., 1941), p. 233.

would fill the void of existence. The "given experience" of transcendental longing is manifested in this play by the absence of identity which destroys the sanity of Taranne. He is progressively stripped of his being, his identity in a series of similar images each representing in its own right and independent of the others the gradual disintegration of the protagonist. The two tableaux are different, yet similar, reinforcing the sameness of man's fate by variation within consistency. It is the Adamovian repetitive structure of intensification, the original statement repeated and intensified by its very repetition with variation. The separate poetic images of the loss of identity do not explain the loss but state it, graphically, scenically, coalescing to create a vivid metaphor of man's hell on earth, of man's nightmarish existence within the confines of time and place.

In the Premier Tableau we first see Taranne deprived of his physical liberty, arrested for exposing himself on a public beach. He asserts his identity as the famous Professeur Taranne but is ignored, not recognized, and rejected by a succession of people — l'Inspecteur en chef, La Journaliste, les Deux Messieurs, La Femme du Monde. Gradually he is being deprived of his illusions, each scene restating his absence of identity. The stage is physically crowded, yet he is alone, for while they all know each other, they do not know him. He speaks into the emptiness of their presence. "Le professeur Taranne a parlé dans le vide, personne ne l'a écouté." [31] We see here a powerfully dramatic depiction of the psychological agony of being alone amongst others, of being separated, alienated in a world not of our creation. The world that Taranne had created in his imagination does not correspond to the reality of his situation. His psychological aloneness is further depicted by the progressive emptying of the stage as each one leaves unnoticed by the others until finally the professor is totally and physically alone. Originally deprived of his physical liberty, his loss of identity and his solitude are now so acute that he prefers the identity of a criminal. He is willing to sign the declaration of guilt.

The continued disintegration of Taranne's world is hinted at by the stage action of La Gérante who now enters while Taranne is alone, rearranges the scenery in silence so that it now depicts a hotel

---

[31] Arthur Adamov, *Le Professeur Taranne* in *Théâtre I* (Paris, 1953), p. 224.

office, and exits silently leaving Taranne once again alone. This bit of transition between the two tableaux prepares us for the further intensification of the sense of absence and aloneness by repetition with slight variation reinforcing the sameness of the dilemma as it unfolds in the Deuxième Tableau. "Les choses viennent toujours par séries," [32] says the Professor, a notion echoed by Adamov himself in his "Note préliminaire" to Théâtre II.

> ... dans cette vie dont les données mêmes sont affreuses, où les situations se répètent fatalement, tout ce que nous pouvons faire, c'est d'abattre, et encore, trop tard, ce que nous prenons abusivement pour l'obstacle réel, le dernier venu de la série maléfique. [33]

And in truth the entire Deuxième Tableau is a restatement, a repetition with modification of the Premier Tableau. Once again Taranne is temporarily deprived of his physical liberty, arrested this time for strewing papers from his note book on the beach. But even the notebook is then revealed to be empty in the middle, and moreover, Taranne cannot even recognize his own handwriting. The police leave once again without his statement of guilt as though he didn't exist. He speaks, but La Gérante is not there and no one listens. Moreover, his key is missing from the board. His sister Jeanne brings him a letter from the rector of the University in Belgium where he claims to have delivered such outstanding courses. This perhaps will be his salvation, his redemption from his most recent ignominies. But his major triumph in life is then negated by this very letter which cites his deficiencies and his plagiarism and refuses to reinvite him to lecture. His sister leaves, the Gérante physically empties the stage, and the professor is now alone with the map which was to place him at the ship's table of honor. The map is blank. Thus the images of the Premier and Deuxième Tableaux are validated by the final image, "une grande surface grise, uniforme, absolument vide." [34] He begins to undress before the total nothingness that is his life, before the total absence of his being.

Each scene of the play makes basically the same statement, each reinforces the others by repetition with variation, each intensifies the

[32] *Le Professeur Taranne*, p. 228.
[33] *Note préliminaire* in *Théâtre II*, p. 11.
[34] *Le Professeur Taranne*, p. 237.

others by the very repetition. The scenes are linked by analogy and not by cause and effect, for nowhere in the play does one scene cause or result from the other. The familiar repetitive structure of intensification of the original absence crushes the protagonist with its persistent, unyielding, machine-like precision.

Taranne is guilty, but of what? He must be exposed, stripped of all illusion and identity, but why? The symmetry of images in the two tableaux is herein revealing. In the Premier Tableau he is guilty of self-exposure, arrested for disrobing on the beach. In the Deuxième Tableau he is arrested for strewing papers from his notebook on the same beach. He has revealed two aspects of himself, the physical and the intellectual, and is condemned for both. In Tableau I he is guilty of excessive self-esteem for he is at first totally unrecognized, unknown, and then confused with the celebrated Professor Ménard. In Tableau II the charge becomes very specifically plagiarism of Professor Ménard's work. In Tableau I he is "guilty" of paranoia when he speaks of the children on the beach.

> Je sais trop bien qu'on m'observe, qu'on me fouille du regard, que tout le monde a les yeux fixés sur moi. Pourquoi me regarde-t-on ainsi? Moi, je ne regarde personne. Le plus souvent, je baisse les yeux. [35]

In the Deuxième Tableau his paranoia is even more acute when he speaks of students, faculty and administration at the Belgian university.

> Ils lui ont écrit, tous! Je savais qu'ils le feraient. Je les ai bien observés. Tandis que je parlais, ils glapissaient (criant d'une voix aiguë): "Il a volé les lunettes du professeur Ménard. Il fait tout comme le professeur Ménard. Dommage qu'il soit plus petit que lui." Et je ne sais quelles balivernes. [36]

But by now, when it is too late and he has been exposed as a fraud, he has gained a degree of insight into his problem, into his identity crisis.

---

[35] *Le Professeur Taranne*, p. 219.
[36] *Le Professeur Taranne*, p. 236.

> Pourquoi me dire ça maintenant, après tant d'années? Pour-
> quoi ne me l'a-t-il pas dit plus tôt? Pourquoi ne me l'ont-ils
> pas dit, tous? Puisque ça se voit! Puisque ça saute aux yeux
> du premier coup. [37]

These images are myriad reflections of his basic "guilt" of non-
identity. His "personality" is rejected in Tableau I by the Inspecteur
en chef, the Journaliste and the Femme du Monde. The closest he
gets to acceptance is a momentary and false recognition as the celebrated Professor Ménard. His non-existence as a true being is made
explicit by the images of a Taranne speaking in a void yet surrounded
by people and by a Taranne totally rejected (the police even neglect
to have him sign the declaration of guilt) and ultimately rejected by
the empty stage. In the Deuxième Tableau he is once again ignored
by the Gérante, neglected by the police, dismissed by the university
as a counterfeit professor, and finally negated by the empty map. All
has been illusion and counterfeit. There has been no real Taranne.
There are no longer even illusions. He has become, as Professor
Lynes suggests, a *mythomane*.

> Only at the end, on reflection, do we fully realize the an-
> guish of the man who must ask such questions of himself,
> the man who has become a *mythomane* in his effort to avoid
> full awareness of the gap between the role he attempts to
> play and his own mediocrity. [38]

In Taranne's lack of identity, in his failure to truly know who he is,
we see his self-imposed image or role as a destroyer of true self, a
growing cancer of non-acceptance. He knows and acts as if he is
guilty, but he is not certain of what. He knows he must expiate, but
is uncertain of why.

The void which Taranne has failed to fill in spite of all his efforts
is but another manifestation of the spiritual absence or void consistently present in Adamov's theater. Taranne's soul-sickness, his sense of
inexplicable guilt, his neurosis of self-humiliation are reflections of his
longing for a dialogue of which he is incapable. He is Man radically alone between a God he does not believe in and a world he cannot
live in.

---

[37] *Le Professeur Taranne*, p. 236.
[38] Lynes, p. 52.

As Taranne is progressively stripped of his identity, A., the protagonist of *Comme nous avons été* is progressively stripped of his manhood, of his independence. The repetitive structure of intensification that informs Adamov's theater once again reveals a central character whose life is characterized by absence, guilt, abortive quest and total disintegration. The obviously different story-line or fable of the two plays yields on examination to a remarkable parallelism and structural similarity. A.'s role as an adult at the opening of the play, like Taranne's as a famous professor, disintegrates within the time and place of the play. As Taranne is finally revealed to be an imposture, a nonentity, A. is finally revealed as a child, controlled, manoeuvred and dominated by his mother. A.'s growth as a man is stunted by a sense of guilt for the death of his father as Taranne's identity is negated by the guilt he feels for assuming another's image. A. is tyrannized and paralyzed into inactivity and eventual childishness by parental "love" as Taranne is thwarted and rendered ineffective by his need for social acceptance. As the family unit of *Comme nous avons été* parallels the societal unity of *Le Professeur. Taranne*, both protagonists, victims of themselves, become victims of "les autres." "L'enfer est l'emprise permanente de tous sur tous." [39]

Comme nous avons été is a short but powerfully dramatic image of modern man's abortive quest for self, a quest denied in this particular case by the castrating mother-figure, by the tyranny of parental love, which is viewed here as one of the oppressions inherent in the human condition itself. It is a familiar theme of Adamov's theater — *L'Invasion, Les Retrouvailles, Le Sens de la Marche* — and while more obvious in these earlier plays, it persists in modified form in the later plays.

The power of this play resides in its apparent but deceptive simplicity, its artful construction which reveals itself slowly as a gesture or a word begins to unite in a thoroughly familiar pattern the three figures and as the story of a man napping on the day he plans to marry coalesces with the story of a mother looking for her lost boy to become the drama of a man eternally lost in the womb of life, never to be free, independent, truly alive.

What we observe take place on the stage — the story that seems to develop or unfold — is but a fragment of the entire, deeper drama

---

[39] *L'Aveu*, p. 89.

which is the play. We see a man, alone, asleep in daytime, awakened by a mother who enters looking for her lost son André. She is joined in the search by la Tante, her sister-in-law. A. is in a hurry to keep an appointment, for he intends to change his life with which he is inexplicably dissatisfied. He is to be married that very day. But slowly and surely la Mère and La Tante dominate the scene, directing the conversation to 1) the lost son André and 2) La Mère's dead husband, André's father, and la Tante's brother. Points of comparison linking André and A. begin to appear: 1) laziness, 2) hiding one's eyes in the hands, 3) the presence of the violin, 4) the saphire ring, 5) the small inheritance, and the two apparently dissimilar dramas begin to mesh. As the mother relates how André used to go to fetch his father from the gambling casino, A. enters into the anecdote as a participating, knowledgeable persona. We now know that he was André, that he is André. The dramatic circle enclosing the three on stage as well as the absence of the dead father is completed by la Tante's gift for André, a toy train, with which the adult A. begins to play. The past begins to move into the present and what was at first extraneous to A.'s need for change in his life has been revealed as the source of powerlessness to effect that very change, as his very condition. As we have been, the play argues, we are. The boy André, under the domination of the powerful mother, had betrayed the father who died by suicide, throwing himself under a train. A. reenacts the scene of their last conversation with its betrayal and guilt, playing both father and son roles, the complete identification is effected, and the man that A. seemed to be at the beginning of the play has been reduced to a helpless child.

The curtain falls on the powerful image of la Mère, triumphant, undressing her man-child and putting him to bed. The aunt, witness to the past and the present, kneeling on all fours, watches the toy train which continues to roll across the floor. But the dynamism of the image is even further intensified by our awareness that this day is not unique, but a drama which has been played out often before and which undoubtedly will be played out again and again. Its very repetition is an integral part of the process of disintegration that characterizes the play's universe. The players know their roles and the precision, timing and uniformity of their movements force us to recognize the deeper level of which the overt action on stage is but a reflection. Adamov himself recognized the importance of repetition in this preliminary note to *Théâtre II*.

> Mais la répétition n'est théâtrale que si les phénomènes qui se répètent tirent leur importance de cette répétition même. [40]

Early in the short play A. feels vaguely guilty for being discovered asleep in the afternoon with the light on.

> Excusez-moi, je suis obligé de sortir. (Il se met à marcher de long en large.) Je ne suis pas libre de mon temps. On ne le dirait pas, n'est-ce pas? (Se tournant vers la Mère.) Vous m'avez trouvé endormi au beau milieu de l'après-midi, alors naturellement vous vous dites: "Celui-là, il n'est pas très occupé, ce ne sont pas les loisirs qui lui manquent." Mais ce n'est pas tout à fait exact. J'ai beaucoup à faire, beaucoup d'obligations. [41]

He had been left a small sum of money and justifies not working on the grounds that he doesn't want to just do anything just to give the impression of living. He is visibly irritated and disturbed by his inertia and lack of independence.

> ça ne va pas durer, mais je suis bien résolu à ne pas attendre le dernier moment pour acquérir une certaine indépendance. [42]

But his failure to work is only a manifestation of a deeper, less recognizable malaise.

> Oui, il faut bien me connaître pour savoir toutes les difficultés que je rencontre ... moi, je ne peux pas. [43]

When the character of A. the apparent adult of the opening part of the play has merged with that of André past and present, we see his dependency and paralysis originating in the child's sense of guilt for the death of the father. He blames himself for not having forseen and prevented the father's suicide.

---

[40] *Note préliminaire* in *Théâtre II*, p. 12.

[41] Arthur Adamov, *Comme nous avons été* in *La Nouvelle Nouvelle Revue Française*, No. 3 (1er mars 1953), p. 434.

[42] *Comme nous avons été*, p. 435.

[43] *Comme nous avons été*, p. 435.

Il (André) aurait dû le savoir. Il n'avait qu'à regarder son père. [44]

This failure of communication between father and son, this failure to act on the part of the child André, stemmed from the tyrannical love-domination of the mother. And what the child was, the man is. For André the man is continually being robbed of his manhood, his independence — and by now "independence" has taken on existential overtones — by the castrating, destroying mother-figure, who daily smothers the child and sterilizes the man into inactivity. A.'s destruction or disintegration is a repetitive structure whose ultimate terms are indicated by la Mère's opening "Excusez-moi monsieur." [45] and closing lines, "C'est sa maman qui le couche pour qu'il fasse dodo." [46]

A.'s attempt to react, to change the order of things, to marry and find a career, to acquire a certain independence are but reflections of the three-dimensional quest to fill the absence of his father, the absence of his manhood, and the absence of his freedom. He knows life as "un état de choses qui ne peut pas s'éterniser," [47] but is incapable of filling the void.

The play stands as a highly concrete metaphor of man's inability to change his human condition, of man's failure to fill the void of his being, of man's insatiable and unfulfilled longing for a lost dimension. Its specific fable of death-back-in-the-womb — A. is psychologically smothered by the mother as the father was driven to suicide — shares points of comparison with *L'Invasion, Le Sens de la Marche* and *Les Retrouvailles* in particulars. But its inner unity or coherence lies in the repetitive structure of intensification that characterizes all of Adamov's work. The play is a day in the life of A., an endless day, a day whose absence of independence, communication, and freedom is part of the human condition itself. Such a play, as Lucien Goldmann points out in his *Jean Racine, Dramaturge,* can be understood and analyzed on its own terms.

Plus l'univers d'une œuvre littéraire est cohérent et plus la relation entre cet univers et la forme dans laquelle il est

---

[44] *Comme nous avons été,* p. 444.
[45] *Comme nous avons été,* p. 431.
[46] *Comme nous avons été,* p. 445.
[47] *Comme nous avons été,* p. 435.

> exprimé est nécessaire, plus aussi l'œuvre est à la fois esthé-
> tiquement valable et facile à analyser en elle-même, en dehors
> de toute référence psychologique et biographique. [48]

Thus, the play stands as a very coherent metaphor of man's lost
spiritual dimension, of his eternal longing, of the soul-sickness in
which we are all participants in varying degrees.

Les Retrouvailles, the last of the "interior-hell" plays, is remark-
ably similar to *Comme nous avons été* not only in its basic structure,
which it shares with all the plays of Adamov, but more specifically
in the parallelism of its two-world syndrome coalescing into one. A. of
Comme nous avons été and Edgar of *Les Retrouvailles* are both incapable of recognizing at first that they are doomed, that the life they
live at the beginning of the play is only an illusion and that it will
be subsumed by the greater drama of which they are a tragic part.
The apparently richer texture of *Les Retrouvailles* results in part
from the degree of awareness evident in the two protagonists. A., the
awakening adult who plans to change his life by marriage is totally
unaware of the larger drama taking place, incapable of recognizing
La Mère as his enemy, incapable of finding in La Mère a concretization of the forces that oppress him. As Adamov says in *Auguste
Strindberg, Dramaturge;*

> Mais au théâtre, comme dans la vie, les puissances sont in-
> carnées par des hommes. [49]

In essence he seems an innocent victim. Edgar, however, is seemingly
conscious of the forces that demand his destruction. The power of this
play lies then in his self-deception, his illusion of victory as he plays
into the hands of the very forces that he thinks he is overpowering
and evading. As the apparently two different worlds of *Comme nous
avons été* (the young man seeking to change his life in marriage and
the mother looking for her lost boy) emerge into one powerful reality,
so the two different worlds of Quevy (Edgar, the mother, and the
fiancée Lina) and that of Montpellier (Edgar, La Plus Heureuse des

---

[48] Goldmann, p. 85.

[49] Arthur Adamov, *Auguste Strindberg, Dramaturge* (Paris, 1955), p. 19.

Femmes, and the fiancée Louise) fuse to demonstrate man's power-lessness before the tyranny of parental love which is but one more manifestation of the tyranny of the human condition, of the forces that oppress us. Both men are helpless before the onslaught, Edgar who seeks to thwart his destruction and A. who is almost totally unaware of it. We see in *Comme nous avons été* and *Les Retrouvailles* one more demonstration of the validity of *La Parodie*, that all destinies are equal, that we are all doomed to the same inevitable failure, or as Adamov says in *L'Aveu,*

Quoiqu'il tente, l'homme se heurte à l'impossible. [50]

In comparison with the classic simplicity of *Comme nous avons été, Les Retrouvailles* is extremely rich in texture. Edgar has left his home village of Quevy to study law at Montpellier. He meets La Plus Heureuse des Femmes and Louise and with their help seeks to break with the dominating influence of the past, betraying his fiancée Lina for Louise. But with time the pattern of the past dominates as he becomes more and more subject to the power of La Plus Heureuse des Femmes who subverts the redemptive force of Louise's love. With Louise now dead in a train accident he returns to Quevy and his mother, there learning of Lina's accidental death by train. As the two dramas merge in his consciousness, he realizes the futility of his struggle, the insidiousness of the human condition, and, paralyzed by fear, he is pushed into a baby coach by the triumphant mother.

The entire action of the short play whose structure is the intensi-fication of Edgar's powerlessness to act, his absence of freedom, is revealed in a series of seven images which unfold in four separate locations — a restaurant, La Plus Heureuse des Femmes's home, a train, la Mère's home. The sequence of this psychological unmasking is relatively unimportant, the principle of causality neatly obviated. For while each separate image is "logical" in its own right, it does not of necessity follow or precede the other. It is this very juxtaposition of the seven logical concrete images whose order is arbitrary which achieves for the play the super-logic or super-reality of dreams, a reality freed of the constrictions of time and place.

---

[50] *L'Aveu,* p. 9.

Thus Edgar's drama to escape from the womb, to achieve being and identity in a life redeemed by love leads back, by way of the binary character Heureuse-Mère, to the womb. As in a dream, the escape is purely illusory. As in a dream, faces and places change from what we thought they were, now seeming to help us, but in the nightmarish reality of the dream, merely helping us to what we had been trying to escape. Adamov's genius in concretizing the personal, subjective nightmares we have all experienced in dreams if not in life is formidable.

The play is then a literal representation of the disintegration of Edgar's dream of reality, of his escape from the womb of the human condition. The illusion he is permitted is temporary and only further intensifies his anguish at the ultimate absence of reality. The true action of the play — his gradual immobilization and eventually total submission, i.e., the disintegration of his personality, his being — is depicted by the gradual coalescence of the two apparently dissimilar worlds ultimately revealed as synonymous. The illusory triangle of victory, escape and freedom

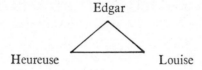

Edgar

Heureuse   Louise

which at first seems to parallel and obviate the triangle of defeat, subjugation and compromise

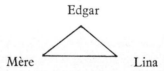

Edgar

Mère   Lina

is ultimately revealed to be the deceptive and destructive triangle of castration.

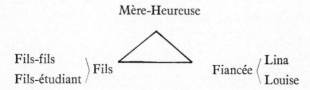

Mère-Heureuse

Fils-fils   ⟩ Fils   Fiancée ⟨ Lina
Fils-étudiant /   \ Louise

The dominant and triumphant mother-figure has had to separate the lovers, for love is capable of destroying her hold on the son. Love is capable of redeeming him from the limitations of his condition. The struggle between mother and lover has been a struggle for Edgar's very soul, a struggle literally and vividly concretized by the two dominant and contrasting images of the conflict, the central and final image of the play.

In the middle of the play as Edgar slowly begins to fall under the domination of La Plus Heureuse des Femmes, justifying his helplessness and absolving himself of guilt and responsibility, Louise sadly watches the accelerating pace of his self-destruction.

> Dès le début de la réplique d'Edgar, Louise est allée à l'avant-scène, à gauche. Elle y est restée, immobile, pleurant, doucement, la brassière à la main. A mesure qu'Edgar parle, la lumière vient de plus en plus sur Louise, laissant Edgar dans le pénombre. Quand Edgar se tait enfin, la scène entière devient presque obscure. [51]

But in sharp contrast to the sympathetic and helpless Louise stands the triumphant, vulgar, laughing La Mère of the final scene who witnesses with apparent glee the last spasms of Edgar's disintegration.

> Edgar, anéanti, titubant, s'appuie des deux mains à la voiture d'enfant. ... La Mère descend du piano, s'approche d'Edgar, et brusquement, avec un rire, l'enfonce dans la voiture d'enfant. Edgar, grotesque, se débat; ses jambes sortent de la voiture. La Mère, riant de plus en plus fort, pousse du pied la voiture, qui traverse la scène de gauche à droite, puis disparaît dans la coulisse. [52]

Thus the smiling, gentle mother putting her adult-child to bed in *Comme nous avons été* and the laughing, violent mother of *Les Retrouvailles* are but two images of the same irresistible force crushing man in his search for freedom and identity.

The structure of the play inexorably propels the gradual then rapid disintegration of Edgar's universe towards its final image. The absence of freedom, identity, self-confidence, and self-definition — his

---

[51] Arthur Adamov, *Les Retrouvailles* in *Théâtre II* (Paris, 1955), p. 90.
[52] *Les Retrouvailles*, p. 94.

psychic impotency — that characterizes Edgar at the beginning of the play is dramatically intensified by a series of structurally similar images until the protagonist is totally and absolutely defeated. Like Pierre, powerless before the lost message of the manuscript, ("On ne voit plus clair."), [53] Edgar is powerless to achieve freedom and identity, ("Je.. je ne m'y retrouve plus!"). [54] His inability to act and react becomes progressively more pronounced and self-perpetuating.

> Provisoire! On dit ça, on se le redit de temps à autre, mais les jours passent... et on se fait tant bien que mal à la situation. Résultat: on ne prend plus aucune mesure pour en sortir et on végète... (riant) éternellement. [55]

Later, when on the train back to Quevy, no longer even capable of safe-guarding his own ticket, he says in protest,

> J'ai perdu mon billet. Je... je ne comprends pas. Je n'ai jamais rien perdu de ma vie. C'est... (criant) la premiere fois. [56]

The pathos of his situation — he is on the way back to his mother, Louise is now dead and he has lost his only hope for salvation — is intensified even further by the irony of his statement. The irony is then compounded when La Plus Heureuse des Femmes "redeems" his loss by buying him another ticket.

> Mais oui, vous me le rendrez! A l'occasion, quand on se reverra. [57]

The truth of the "on se reverra" has been skillfully prepared throughout the play by the gradual fusion of the two triangles of identity which in turn has been enhanced by the parallelism of the corresponding motifs: the trains, the bicycles, the pianos, and finally the sewing machine with the baby coach.

The play is a metaphor of man's futile protest against the tyranny of parental love and the human condition. Edgar's attempt at revolt,

---

[53] *L'Invasion*, p. 77.
[54] *Les Retrouvailles*, p. 77.
[55] *Les Retrouvailles*, p. 80.
[56] *Les Retrouvailles*, p. 92.
[57] *Les Retrouvailles*, p. 93.

his essay at escape was but a short-lived, vain illusion whose cruelty is made all the more demonic by the final grotesque, abortive struggle to extricate himself from the baby carriage. It is a world, as George E. Wellwarth suggests in his *The Theater of Protest and Paradox*, wherein cruelty becomes an almost tangible entity.

> He (Adamov) protests against the merciless cruelty of the world, a cruelty that is at once inhuman and superhuman, omnipresent in the external and immanent in the individual, inner world, an almost tangible entity in itself and at the same time an emmanation of a greater, instinctively malicious entity. [58]

In *Les Retrouvailles* as in all four "interior-hell" plays, man's existence is portrayed as absence, as a void to be filled, rendered by the barest and most existential of images whose sole purpose is to posit the powerlessness of man in a hostile universe that has lost its redeeming spiritual dimension. This underlying absence, of which each play is but a variant image, is almost entirely stripped in these plays of political and social ingredients, relatively freed of the limitations of time and place. The accent is on the psychic impotency of man, objectified on the stage, rendered concrete and dramatic by a series of similar images, variations on the predominant obsession or absence. Thus while the texture of each play varies, the repetitive structure of intensification of man's absence, persists. His spiritual malaise remains unredeemable in a world strangled by its attempt at prayer. Life in the universe of these plays, like the life Adamov knew in the concentration camp of Argelès, is hell, and hell is absence.

> Le camp ce fut pour moi l'enfer, c'est-à-dire l'absence. [59]

---

[58] George E. Wellwarth, *The Theater of Protest and Paradox* (New York, 1964), p. 28.

[59] *L'Aveu,* p. 146.

CHAPTER II

THE POLICE-STATE PLAYS

The four "police-state" plays, *La Parodie, La grande et la petite manœuvre, Le Sens de la Marche,* and *Tous contre Tous* share the same time period as the "interior-hell" plays — all were written between 1947 and 1953, i.e., before *Le Ping-Pong* — just as they share the unifying syntagmatic axis or structural invariant. Moreover, Adamov, as well as most of his commentators, has insisted on the formal and thematic unity of all eight plays, characterizing this as his early avant-garde theater of the absurd period in contrast to the later "political" and more "realistic" plays.

But this traditional, "dual-orientation" understanding of Adamov's theater is predicated upon the notion that the later plays do not fit the mold of the earlier plays, that there is a shift or reorientation in form and thematic content from *La Parodie* to *Off limits.* We prefer, however, to recognize that within the unity of Adamov's entire work each play or group of plays is a variation of each other, that within the temporal unfolding of his work there are spatial paradigms, that these paradigms are informational, revealing that the more apparent developments of the later chronological period exist in germ form within the earlier plays, that in fact there is ultimately a unifying, but of necessity abstract, syntagmatic axis.

In the theater of Adamov man is condemned to the absence of and the separation from a unifying dimension which we have called spiritual. His internal suffering or existential anguish, the disunity within, prevents him from communicating with others. Each individual exists as an isolated island, suffering alone, incapable of resolving the destructive interior conflict of his condition. A victim of himself, he becomes a victim of others, as well as a persecutor of others. The two oppressions, interior and exterior, are of the same essence and coexist simultaneously, the one reflecting the other, the one oppression varying in intensity and emphasis from play to play but never eliminating the other. The unity of the twofold dilemma remains intact throughout Adamov's entire theater.

In contrast to the almost exclusively private "hell" of *L'Invasion*, *Le Professeur Taranne*, *Comme nous avons été*, and *Les Retrouvailles*, the "police-state" plays demonstrate more emphatically the dual oppression that modern man faces, the emptiness within as well as the separation from others which will predominate in the later "political" and "social" plays. The action of all four plays, their disorder within, is played out against a "police-state" background which reveals early in the theater of Adamov a deep social concern and political orientation which, as Leonard Pronko points out in his *Avant-Garde. The Experimental Theater in France,* distinguishes Adamov from his contemporaries Beckett and Ionesco.

> The police state plays, however, ... already betray a social awareness and a political turn of mind. No matter how abstract they become, the characters are not inhabitants of the non-political universe of Ionesco, or of the asocial one of Beckett. On the contrary, they belong to a state that controls, dominates, and oppresses them, and they are aware of the social relationships existing between the people within the State, whether they be political leaders and refugees, or fathers and sons. [1]

La Parodie, while in a certain sense, the most abstract and negative of Adamov's plays, is grounded in an atmosphere of exterior oppression. The sights and sounds of a modern police-state are more than just the dominant and repressive background against which the drama takes place. They are rather part of the destructive action of the play, symbolic of the totalitarianism of a human condition experienced without recourse to the lost spiritual dimension. The entire play is a trial and judgement of a world gone absurd, of a life that is in truth a parody of life. The common hell of this world permits of no escape,

---

[1] Leonard Cabell Pronko, *Avant-Garde. The Experimental Theater in France* (Berkeley and Los Angeles, 1964), p. 137.

for the hell is within as well as in others, the exterior political suppression just one more concrete manifestation of man's degradation.
Adamov's characters, as Jean Duvignaud suggests, have only one
story to tell.

> Condamnés à souffrir comme des victimes entre les mains
> du bourreau, les créatures d'Adamov n'ont autre histoire que
> celle de leur dégradation. [2]

All roads in this play lead to degradation and ultimate destruction,
and each character is but an interchangeable figure on a descending
scale.

The play has little apparent plot. Two men, N and the Employé,
both seek in their own way and fail to receive help of one sort or
another from Lili. We see them at various stages of futility and of
physical and psychological disintegration until by the end of the play
N is dead and the Employé is in jail as Lili goes off with the Directeur. But the real statement of the play, divided rather evenly
into twelve short tableaux in two parts with a prologue, is the futility
of man in an absurd universe, his powerlessness to effect change, his
inability to direct his destiny by choice. The two protagonists seem
to choose different routes to salvation at the beginning of the play.
N seems to accept defeat, but in truth seeks completion in death at
the hands of Lili, a kind of deliverance.

> Je n'ai pas choisi de vivre, mais si je pouvais choisir ma
> mort . . . (Pause.) Vous m'aviez promis de me tuer, tuez-moi. [3]

The Employé, on the other hand, struggles for life and love. His
newly found city,

> Cette rue ne ressemble à aucune autre, elle ne me rappelle
> rien. Il y a là un cinéma et des arbres devant. Les arbres
> sont une promesse de résurrection. [4]

his pursuit of a career and his interest in the woman Lili are indicative
of a man who still knows hope.

---

[2] Jean Duvignaud, "Le Théâtre d'Adamov," *Nouvelle Nouvelle Revue
Française*, No. 22 (Oct. 54), p. 729.

[3] Arthur Adamov, *La Parodie* in *Théâtre I* (Paris, 1953), p. 17.

[4] *La Parodie*, p. 12.

> Voyez-vous, je cherche depuis toujours une vraie ville où la
> vie serait gaie et les gens de bonne humeur. J'étais sûr
> qu'elle existait quelque part; je me réjouis de l'avoir trouvée. [5]

Both men in fact seek a meaning to life, the fulfillment of a promise,
N a promise of death at the hands of Lili, the Employé a promise
of a "resurrection" mediated by the woman Lili. Woman becomes, as
Richard Sherrell points out, an agent of self-investigation.

> In Adamov's self-exorcism he must plumb his own depths in
> order to find the meaning or the sense of his separation.
> In this process woman becomes the agent of self-investiga-
> tion, and as such, woman symbolizes both the attraction of
> death (with attendant fears of castration) and the possibility
> of renewal. [6]

Both men are frustrated in their quest, both are continually degraded
and ultimately destroyed. It is as if both N and the Employé were
the fulfillment of each other, the one guilty of despair, the other of
hope. At one point in the 5ᵉ Tableau the Employé raises his hand to
strike N for not remaining awake while on watch for Lili. But N
raises his own hand.

> Il lève le bras dans le pose exacte du bras de l'Employé, le
> laisse un instant dans cette pose, puis s'en frappe violem-
> ment le visage. Au même instant, l'Employé laisse retomber
> son bras. Donner l'impression que le bras de N s'est substitué
> à celui de l'Employé. [7]

In the Première Partie N appears continually weaker each time
he appears on stage, his disintegration much more apparent than that
of the Employé who continually shows signs of energy and possibility.
He permits himself the illusion of salvation in the form of Lili, always
certain of her eventual arrival. But she does not come. Thus both
men are rejected by the same woman, by the only person named in
the play, by the only force capable of redeeming others.

---

[5] *La Parodie*, p. 28.

[6] Richard E. Sherrell, "Arthur Adamov and Invaded Man," *Modern
Drama*, 7 (1965: 399-404), pp. 400-401.

[7] *La Parodie*, p. 30.

The six tableaux of the Seconde Partie are a restatement in intensified form of the vision of the Première Partie, of the helplessness of man in a world that is a parody of true life. The Employé, rejected by the redeeming life-force of Woman, is now older, less energetic, less well-dressed, less self-confident, incapable of working and eventually humiliated by jail. N, whose deterioration was so much more advanced and obvious in the Première Partie, is seen as progressively more helpless and confused, even incapable of distinguishing the celebrated Lili from the Pauvre Prostituée, and finally as dead, as debris swept from the stage. This accelerating pace of disintegration reveals the vision of the play, that in time all effort will prove abortive, that each man in his time and turn is destined for total destruction, that N is merely the nth. degree of a scale on which all are figures.

The repetitive structure of intensification which informs the play circulates around the central figure of Lili, the image of Woman as a redemptive force. In the Première Partie Lili is pictured as a kind of magnet or force in constant circular motion that draws all within reach into its field infusing it with life or power. She is the only person named in the play. She is the only one who really laughs. She is constantly in motion drawing everyone to her by the force and sweep of her action. Others seem to gain strength from her. The Directeur says of her,

> Dès qu'elle me quitte, mes forces m'abandonnent. [8]

Later, when speaking of the newspaper, he indicates her sustaining role.

> Plus de Lili, plus d'"Avenir". [9]

The Journaliste, perhaps the only one not dominated by her power, recognizes its force in others. He asks N,

> Quand vous êtes séparé d'elle depuis un certain temps, votre état physique change, n'est-ce pas, vous êtes nerveux, agité sans raison, couvert de sueurs... [10]

---

[8] *La Parodie*, p. 22.
[9] *La Parodie*, p. 23.
[10] *La Parodie*, p. 32.

N, the most obviously humiliated and subjugated character of the play, feels that it is she alone who can fill the void within.

> Mais je suis si vide, si perdu. Où est-elle? [11]

It is as though Lili is at the core of life, a power radiating out, keeping all in orbit by the very force of her circular action.

But by the Second Tableau her power to hold all in orbit begins to weaken. She no longer laughs, she shows signs of slowing down physically on stage, she is revealed as less and less capable of sustaining the parody of life in which she has become a substitute for the lost sustaining dimension. And she herself is slowly being made aware of her limitations. As she becomes less and less confident, she protests.

> Comme je suis malheureuse! Les gens que j'aime me font des affronts abominables. Il lui a dit qu'Antoine pouvait vivre très vieux, même si je l'abandonnais. Je n'ai pas compris. Ils prétendent que le journal continuerait de paraître. Comme si "Demain" pouvait exister sans moi ... Les hommes mentent, c'est inimaginable. [12]

But *La Parodie* is a world in which it makes no difference, where all ends in nothingness, degradation, despair, and dissolution. And even the life-force Lili that keeps the whole thing spinning becomes worn out, mechanical, meaningless. At the end Lili must go as the eternal prostitute to the Directeur and leave behind her real love, the Journaliste. It is a world where all must suffer, where N is only the nth. degree of humiliation, where death is the final humiliation towards which we all progress.

Yet with all of its meaninglessness the universe of *La Parodie* is still subject to the laws of time and place. Time does pass, people get older looking, the trees' leaves yellow and as time elapses, it becomes more important. The clock without hands has become much bigger than in the Première Partie. The future is more rapidly devoured. The accelerated pace of time coincides with the intensification that is the play's structure as the newspaper "L'Avenir" of the Première Partie becomes the "Demain" in the Seconde Partie.

---

[11] *La Parodie,* p. 33.
[12] *La Parodie,* p. 38.

As time becomes increasingly important, so does space. The world becomes more oppressive as it closes in. The dance hall of the Première Partie has shrunk as the world of *La Parodie* moves in on its people and suffocates them.

> Il s'est rétréci, le décor n'occupe que le milieu de la scène. [13]

The same people, the same pairing off, but now time, as it passes, passes more quickly and movement becomes more and more restricted as Man becomes progressively more a prisoner of his own categories. Unnamed, geographically free of specifics, this no-man's land is the modern police-state city where, as Roger Blin suggests, the great questions are silenced.

> C'est la ville d'affres qui étouffe mieux qu'aucun autre lieu la grande Interrogation. Toutes les rues mouillées se ressemblent... Un homme chassé et un homme qui cherche, marchent pareil. [14]

It is the extension of the oppression, lack of communication, and emptiness of the individuals who inhabit it. In this play as in others of the "police-state" plays, the specifics of social and political oppression are not spelled out. It is rather the frightening notion of social and political oppression as an extension of ourselves and our limitations that is highlighted. The State as an abstraction of the horror that man permits is in focus and keenly felt throughout the play. There are constant allusions in both dialogue and stage directions to mass arrests, whistles, searchlights, noises. It is definitely the modern police state because the accent is on the "désordre qui règne ces temps-ci," [15] "dans cette époque troublée," [16] where "ce n'est plus comme avant." [17] Resolutions of repression and the closing of the churches speak to us however abstractly of the modern period wherein the marionnette-like

---

[13] *La Parodie*, p. 48.

[14] Roger Blin in Arthur Adamov, *La Parodie, L'Invasion,* précédées d'une lettre d'André Gide, et des témoignages de René Char, Jacques Prévert, Henri Thomas, Jacques Lemarchand, Jean Vilar, Roger Blin (Paris, 1950), p. 18.

[15] *La Parodie*, p. 23.

[16] *La Parodie*, p. 34.

[17] *La Parodie*, p. 43.

behavior of the characters are indicative of an age of conformity and social repression. It is, as Carlos Lynes points out, not life but the parody of life that we are viewing.

> This play is, of course, the *parody* of meaningful human life; when it is over, we may suspect that we too are living just such a parody. [18]

The theme of absence, so central to the theater of Adamov, reaches its most total statement in *La Parodie*, where the absence portrayed is the very absence of life itself. What we see so graphically on the stage is a literal demonstration in theatrical terms of life lived according to the dialectics of parody. The text itself, as Robert Champigny demonstrates in *Le Genre dramatique*, is but a schematic, a guide or outline for production, only one of the many elements constituting the language of theater. It begs for scenic space.

> De fait, il faut admettre qu'une pièce de théâtre ne peut atteindre sa pleine mesure qu'à la représentation. Spectateur et acteur sont nécessaires à son accomplissement. Le texte de la pièce ne fournit qu'un schéma. Il a l'air d'un roman inachevé, d'un roman où seules les citations en style direct auraient été mises au net. Prendre la pièce lue comme base de notre analyse, ce serait manquer l'originalité du genre dramatique. [19]

Adamov claims that as a playwright, as an artist dealing in that very special language which is the language of theater — text, staging, actors, direction, audience — there is always one special scene towards which he directs the entire play. [20] He specifically states that with *Le Ping-Pong* he even began writing the play after he had conceived the final scene wherein two old men play ping-pong.

> Je ne savais pas encore quel en serait le sujet, et déjà j'avais décidé qu'il se terminerait par une partie de ping-pong entre deux vieillards. [21]

---

[18] Carlos Lynes, Jr., "Adamov or 'Le sens littéral' in the theater," *Yale French Studies*, No. 14 (Winter 1954-55), p. 53.

[19] Robert Champigny, *Le Genre dramatique* (Monte-Carlo, 1965), p. 15.

[20] Arthur Adamov, *Auguste Strindberg, Dramaturge* (Paris, 1955), p. 7.

[21] Arthur Adamov, *Note préliminaire* in *Théâtre II* (Paris, 1955), p. 15.

But even without this information, it is apparent that the dramaturgy of Adamov is such that he seeks to leave his audience with powerful images of man being crushed by both the exterior and interior forces of life and that among these powerful images there is frequently one very special and very concrete image of man totally helpless, of man ultimately at the mercy of others and of the human condition. Perhaps it is Adamov after all who has most successfully dramatized the ideas of Artaud.

> Je propose donc un théâtre où des images physiques broient et hypnotisent la sensibilité du spectateur pris dans le théâtre comme dans un tourbillon de forces supérieures. Un théâtre qui, abandonnant la psychologie, raconte l'extraordinaire, mette en scène des conflits naturels, des forces naturelles et subtiles, et qui se présente d'abord comme une force exceptionnelle de dérivation. [22]

Taranne undressing, the boy-man André being put to bed by his mother, Edgar struggling futilely in the baby carriage, N being swept off stage are all very concrete images of man being destroyed.

La grande et la petite manœuvre, perhaps the best early synthesis of the dual dilemma of man, builds in increasing intensity toward its final image of a legless, armless cripple being pushed out the door into the turbulent street by the very woman in whom he had most faith and who represented to him his only possible means of salvation.

As the play begins, two men, later identified as Le Mutilé and le Militant, are manhandled and beaten by the police. Le Mutilé claims that he is not part of the Movement, a group determined to overthrow the totalitarian government of the state, but carries the wounded Militant home to safety. They are brothers-in-law, but have little else in common. The Militant actively combats the oppression of the totalitarian police-state in which they live. Like the Employé of *La Parodie* the Militant is an apostle of hope, resurrection and change. In contrast Le Mutilé, like N, is passive, more cynical, defeated, though still indignant at man's victimization. While he believes that his brother-in-law is following the wrong course, that he is incapable

---

[22] Antonin Artaud, *Le Théâtre et son Double* (Paris, 1964), p. 126.

of effecting change, Le Mutilé is outraged at the treatment Le Militant
receives and says to his sister;

> Je ne le défends pas. Je sais, il se trompe, il ne pourra rien
> changer à ce monde. Mais eux n'ont pas le droit. [23]

The "eux," as in *La Parodie,* are not a specific government or form
of oppression, but rather an abstraction of man's manipulation of
others and his inhumanity toward fellow man. The Mutilé recognizes
the futility of resistance and obeys the mechanical voices of the
Monitors which are acoustically omnipresent and which represent
the control of the state over those who permit themselves to be subjugated. Each time that they call to him we see him visibly shaken
on stage, slavishly following their commands. The interior disintegration of the Mutilé, his loss of freedom, his surrender of choice and
desire, is dramatized by his progressive physical mutilation. In the
Première Partie he loses his arms, in the Seconde Partie his legs.
Reduced to moving about in a small cart, he is at the mercy of all,
but especially of Erna, for he somehow feels that if he can have
total faith in her, he will escape the prison of his existence.

> Oui, désormais, je penserai à vous, sans cesse, très fort, si
> fort... si fort que peut-être ils me laisseraient en paix. [24]

This prison of existence is of course both the "petite" and the "grande
manœuvre" of the play, a dual hell of personal and political dimensions. The oppressive, totalitarian regime that crushes him and before
which he exhibits passive indignation is but the extension of the
"police-state" mentality of his soul. Because he is incapable of love,
of always thinking of her, he forgets and even doubts her, and is
thereby subject to further physical degradation. The two dimensions
of private and public, interior and exterior, metaphysical and social,
existential and political in which we all live mesh on stage in the
image of the Mutilé, helpless, abandoned, betrayed, the redemptive-
force Erna sadistically pushing him in his cart out into the street and
total destruction.

---

[23] Arthur Adamov, *La grande et la petite manœuvre* in *Théâtre I* (Paris,
1953), p. 106.
[24] *La grande et la petite manœuvre,* p. 113.

But in this world no one escapes. The Militant who actively resists oppression by combating it is also crushed by the same oppression, only more subtly. The Resistance defeats the regime and becomes the regime, becomes the oppressive "eux" against which it had fought. The Militant's interior disintegration — he is willing to sacrifice his wife, the child, people in general for an abstract cause — is visually portrayed in his victory speech in the 9th Tableau. While arguing that the demands of the future are such that inevitably some will suffer and even unjustly, while his words speak of courage, strength, hope and growth, he physically collapses. The image gives the lie to his words. Oppression has won by a strategy of defeat. For it matters little who the agents of oppression are as long man remains its victim.

While *La Parodie* presents oppression as an abstract but destructive force, *La grande et la petite manœuvre* presents resistance and revolution as an abstract but fruitless antidote. Moreover, as Geneviève Serreau points out in her *Histoire du "nouveau théâtre,"* this play signifies perhaps better than any other of the early theater Adamov's dual concerns.

> Dès *La grande et la petite manœuvre,* et dans la tradition de l'expressionisme allemand, Adamov mêle les préoccupations politiques à la description de son univers intérieur. [25]

Woman, who represents perhaps the only redeeming value in the early plays, becomes less central in this play, yet more destructively active. While Lili of *La Parodie* fails to redeem the men within her orbit and becomes progressively more passive, Erna is from her first appearance on stage progressively crueler and more debilitating. Like Lili she still believes that Woman is at the center of the universe, that she must be needed, but she expresses now a lurid interest in the Mutilé's physical mutilation and previous sex life.

> ça ne me gêne pas du tout qu'un homme n'ait pas de mains. Pourvu que, moi, j'aie les miennes. (Elle rit.) On se débrouille. [26]

She takes sadistic pleasure as Neffer recounts how the regime tortures prisoners, is overly curious about the movements of the Militant and

---

[25] Geneviève Serreau, *Histoire du "nouveau theatre"* (Paris, 1966), p. 71.
[26] *La grande et la petite manœuvre,* p. 112.

about why the Mutilé must always leave her. In the 7ᵉ Tableau we see her falsely jealous of La Sœur.

> Je me trompais. Il y a une femme qui veut toujours de toi: ta sœur. C'est elle que tu vas retrouver? Avoue-le. [27]

As the Mutilé struggles to leave, she tears his crutches from him, and Woman the Redemptor becomes Woman the eternal nemesis. "Allons, un petit effort!" [28] In the final Tableau, when once again the Mutilé, now a *cul-de-jatte,* must leave, she suspects him of bad faith and becomes his agent of persecution and death.

> Décidément tu nous quittes. Tu veux défiler avec les autres, célébrer la victoire! (Pause.) Mais, prends garde, on pourrait t'écraser. Tu tiens si peu de place! (Erna, riant aux éclats, qui disparaît à droite dans la coulisse.) [29]

In a play wherein irony abounds, this is perhaps the major irony, that man's gradual degradation and destruction is ultimately intensified and completed by the very forces which seem to offer him escape and salvation. The Militant is destroyed by the Revolution as the Mutilé is crushed by the Woman Redemptor. The play's repetitive structure of intensification further parallels that of *La Parodie* in that man's posture of reaction to the oppressive forces of life is divided into two characters, the Mutilé of passive indignation and the Militant of active revolution. That one seems to be destroyed while the other has the illusion of escaping the political oppression (la petite manœuvre) is further testimony to the unity and coherence of the play's structure. For it is the very dominance on the political level — or the illusion of that dominance — that ultimately destroys the Militant on the metaphysical level (la grande manœuvre). The structure of the play is a merciless, devastating intensification by repetition with variation of the absence of love and human compassion which permits man's oppression on both the political and metaphysical dimensions. And as Jean Duvignaud points out, the play defines the essence of modern suffering.

---

[27] *La grande et la petite manœuvre,* p. 131.
[28] *La grande et la petite manœuvre,* p. 131.
[29] *La grande et la petite manœuvre,* p. 141.

> La plus belle des pièces d'Adamov, *La grande et la petite manœuvre*, offre justement une image visuelle de la douleur. . . . Cette pièce, sans doute, l'une des plus originales de la scène moderne, incarne une dialectique tragique d'un genre nouveau: condamnée au supplice d'être consciente, la conscience se dégrade; la terreur qui la ronge grandit sa part de lucidité sans jamais la hausser à ses propres yeux. Ici, Adamov fixe l'essence de la souffrance moderne: l'homme déchu glisse sur la pente savonneuse. Son malheur vient de ce qu'il se mutile avec une sorte de joie dès qu'il sent sa défaite irréductible. [30]

Of all of the early plays *La grande et la petite manœuvre* succeeds best in realizing dramatically Adamov's conception of a new theater which sought to reveal the spiritual through the direct, concrete, and literal representation of man and his dilemma. This "new" dramatic language which seeks to utilize all elements of the theater — text, sight, gesture, sound, lighting, music — is indebted to Artaud's concept of theater as a "fête" or rite which appeals first to the physical so that it might later speak better to the spiritual. The play's attraction, as Bernard Dort suggests, is in its celebration of destruction.

> L'attrait (ou la révulsion) que cette pièce suscite chez le spectateur est, au premier chef, physique: bruits lancinants, cris, soudaineté des événements, brutalité des rapports scéniques des personnages. Le théâtre retrouve par là la mission que lui assignait Antonin Artaud: d'être une fête, une fête de destruction. [31]

It is also highly indebted, like most of French contemporary theater, to the experimentations of film and of certain film directors seeking to create a unique or autonomous language, a language not translatable into any other art form. Jean Duvignaud in his *Sociologie du Théâtre* speaks of film as having a purifying effect on contemporary theater.

> En forçant le théâtre à retrouver ses principes les plus simples et les plus authentiques le cinéma a contraint la création dramatique à se dépouiller des justifications, explications

---

[30] Duvignaud, p. 732.

[31] Bernard Dort, "Les pièces d'Adamov," *Les Temps modernes*, No. 63 (janv. 51), p. 1137.

> idéologiques latentes qui s'attachaient aux personnages "psychologiques," à éliminer les allégories et les symboles afin de présenter une image *littérale* de l'homme. [32]

The play, in a certain sense, imitates film, juxtaposing in rapid succession exterior or public scenes with interior or private scenes. Most scenes or tableaux are separated only by a moment of darkness or emptiness of stage, and it is only the two major parts of the play which are divided by the traditional curtain. Adamov's production note,

> Les tableaux doivent se succéder presque instantanément. Enchaînement quasi cinématographique. [33]

further indicates the effect desired. It is an effect in keeping with a vision of man as dislocated, his history fragmented and non sequential, his unity splintered, his existence apparently absurd. It is this spiritual awareness that Adamov's theater celebrates in a rite of expiation and self-discovery. By appealing first to the physical, the theater of Adamov attains the "univers spirituel" that Henri Gouhier speaks of as necessary in his *Le Théâtre et L'Existence.*

> Le monde du drame n'est pas seulement l'univers physique auquel le corps appartient: c'est aussi et surtout l'univers spirituel qui enveloppe les âmes. Pas de monde sans une vision du monde et sans une image de l'homme dans le monde. [34]

Repetition in the theater of Adamov is not merely a device or technique. It is rather that formal element which conveys best his vision of a world in which man must battle a continuing series of obstacles knowing, in varying degrees, that these "obstacles" are merely concrete symbols of the real battle or loss, the absence of a spiritual or unifying dimension. Adamov speaks of this damaging series of obstacles in the preliminary note to his *Théâtre II.*

> ... dans cette vie dont les données mêmes sont affreuses, où les situations se répètent fatalement, tout ce que nous pouvons

---

[32] Jean Duvignaud, *Sociologie du Théâtre* (Paris, 1965), p. 547.
[33] *La grande et la petite manœuvre*, p. 102.
[34] Henri Gouhier, *Le Théâtre et L'Existence* (Paris, 1952), p. 29.

faire, c'est d'abattre, et encore, trop tard, ce que nous prenons abusivement pour l'obstacle réal, le dernier venu de la série maléfique. [35]

The repetitive structure of intensification which informs the theater of Adamov is most apparent, and therefore perhaps least effective, in *Le Sens de la Marche*. The play is divided into four acts with a Prologue, each act a variation of the Prologue, each act a repetition of the statement contained in the Prologue. It is as if Adamov consciously sought to achieve the poetry of variation that he so astutely recognized as central to the theater of Strindberg.

La poésie, dans le théâtre de Strindberg, naît de la répétition, ou plutôt de la demi-répétition, du parallélisme qui n'en est pas tout à fait un, de la variation légère des premiers motifs. [36]

In the Prologue Henri, the protagonist of the play, is torn between revolutionary action and a sort of domestic tranquility. He fails to leave with his two comrades from the Resistance, Georges and Albert, remaining in the home of his tyrannical father, despising his totally submissive sister Mathilde, and yet loving Lucile who is equally submissive to her father, the Prédicateur. The structure of the play moves towards a gradual, then rapid disintegration of the play's universe. The disintegration comes from the intensification by repetition of the prevailing absence, an absence of identity as an independent agent. Henri's inability to act is played out in the three dominant arenas of life — 1. the military (Act 1, La Caserne), 2. the church (Act II, La Secte), and 3. the school (Act III, L'Ecole).

He fails to escape the tyranny of parental love in all three situations where 1. the Commandant, 2. the Prédicateur, and 3. the Directeur de l'Ecole are merely variations of the powerful father-figure. Nor can he escape the debilitating influence of Woman whom he continually chooses over action and commitment to the revolution. Act IV, "La Chambre du Père," is a sort of epilogue, a concluding section that rounds out the design of the play. Henri is once again at home, a failure in all his efforts toward meaningful action. But the

[35] *Note préliminaire* in *Théâtre II,* p. 11.
[36] *Strindberg,* p. 62.

ignominy of his situation, the disintegration of his universe, the degradation resulting from his failure to act are all crystalized for him by the appearance of Berne, his father's former masseur, as a replacement in the parental triangle from which he had vainly sought to escape. In a final, dying spasm of revolt Henri strangles Berne.

The theme of parental love as an oppressive force inherent in human existence, which was treated in *Comme nous avons été* and *Les Retrouvailles,* takes on in this play an added dimension. Henri's absence of independence, his failure to react against parental pressure, his inability to free himself from domination results in his failure to become a revolutionary against political oppression. The one is an extension of the other. The order that his father prizes so highly in the home parallels the totalitarian notion of order in the State, an order admitting of no foreign or corrupting influence, a restrictive and suppressive order that prefers tranquility to truth, flattery to communication.

> Ce qu'il faut, c'est étouffer le mal dans le germe, ce n'est pas permettre... Est-ce qu'il y a du remue-ménage dans ma maison? Est-ce qu'il y a des mécontents? [37]

It is an "order" echoed by the Commandant, "Qu'est-ce que je vois? Un désordre pareil!," [38] restated by the Prédicateur, "C'était... la présence étrangère." [39] and finally summed up the Directeur de L'Ecole, "La plaisanterie a assez duré, Messieurs." [40] Coaxed and coached by the Adjoint, Henri himself, when once in a position of apparent authority, wavers and begins to assume the same totalitarian attitudes.

> C'est vrai, il y a ici un tel désordre. C'est peut-être à cause de ça... en partie... [41]

But finally, it is Berne in the closing moments of the play who brings the circle of containment to its conclusion. "Il faut tout de même assurer l'ordre, mon petit." [42] It is this circle of debilitating authority

---

[37] Arthur Adamov, *Le Sens de la Marche* in *Théâtre II* (Paris, 1955), pp. 23-24.
[38] *Le Sens de la Marche,* p. 35.
[39] *Le Sens de la Marche,* p. 43.
[40] *Le Sens de la Marche,* p. 59.
[41] *Le Sens de la Marche,* p. 53.
[42] *Le Sens de la Marche,* p. 63.

and conformity from which Henri makes a final effort to escape by killing Berne. And it is this very act which distinguishes Henri from A. of *Comme nous avons été* and Edgar of *Les Retrouvailles* of the "interior-hell" plays. Berne, like the Commandant, the Prédicateur and the Directeur, represents not only the father-figure, but the social and political establishment against which Henri had sought to fight, against which he now makes a final, spasmodic gesture of defiance.

Paralleling the domination and oppression of the father-figure is the tyranny of the beloved, the destructive Woman, who throughout this play paralyzes Henri's thrust towards fulfillment, independence, and action. In the Prologue he fails to leave with the Resistance because of her. In Act I he hesitates to escape from the prison of barracks life because she has arranged for him to work for the Secte under the tyrannical directorship of her father. In Act III he has become a professor for her and for her alone. Only on learning of the death of his comrade Georges at the hands of the opposition does he dare break from the limitations of their relationship.

> (*Repoussant brutalement Lucile.*) Non, je ne veux plus! C'est fini, je n'ai plus l'âge. (*Criant à tue-tête:*) Va-t-en! [43]

But both the parental and female dominations are only symptomatic of a vaguely felt and less obvious flaw, an infinite suffering of which these dominations and the particular situations of the play are but concrete manifestations, an absence or void which military, church, professional and sentimental life cannot fill. It is the void of indecision. Henri is never really certain of his motives. Like A. of *Comme nous avons été* who vaguely feels dissatisfied with his life and seeks to change it by marriage, Henri wants to flee the parental tyranny of home and fight oppression and injustice within the State. But he can't. "Je ne peux pas m'en aller! Pas maintenant." [44] It is a motif endlessly repeated throughout the play. He wants to act, but each time the occasion presents itself, he seems paralyzed and afraid, continually postponing his action. In the Prologue he wants to leave his father and go away with Lucile, but he feels powerless.

---

[43] *Le Sens de la Marche*, p. 58.
[44] *Le Sens de la Marche*, p. 24.

> De toutes façons, je ne resterai pas. Si ce n'est pas au-
> jourd'hui, alors, demain . . . [45]

When he is in the prison of military life, he wants to escape the
nightmare of his existence, but fails to flee.

> Mais ce cauchemar va finir, Mathilde. (*Il s'arrête.*) De-
> main . . .[46]

Later, when comfortably protected in the Secte, he feels guilt and
remorse, but does not leave.

> Lucile, je veux te parler. Il faut que je parte, c'est trop
> honteux. Pendant que je fais le concierge à la Secte, il y a
> des hommes qui continuent la lutte, qui risquent leur vie,
> pour que d'autres plus tard en profitent, pour qu'eux, au
> moins, n'étouffent pas . . . [47]

His original failure to take action — not joining Georges and Albert
in the Resistance — is also at the same time a failure to break the
bonds of parental tyranny. The political or exterior conflict coalesces
with the psychological or interior conflict to create a feeling of guilt
that haunts him throughout the play.

> Pourquoi ne les ai-je pas rejoints tous deux? [48]

Thus the play, like all four of the "police state" plays mixes intensely
the dual concerns of Adamov. Failure to act on a political level (The
Resistance) is an extension of Henri's failure to act on a psychological
level (Family and Lover) which are in turn concrete images of the
failure to act itself, the paralysis of the will, the absence of action
on the existential level. The entire play with its ceaseless variations
is a rendering in concrete and literal images of a psychological state
of impotence and a spiritual state of despair.

In the closing scene of the play Berne sums up the entire action
up to that point when he welcomes home the prodical son.

---

[45] *Le Sens de la Marche,* p. 31.
[46] *Le Sens de la Marche,* p. 34.
[47] *Le Sens de la Marche,* p. 44.
[48] *Le Sens de la Marche,* p. 55.

> Toi, c'est autre chose, tu t'es lancé dans les aventures, l'amour, les études... Enfin, on se retrouve, c'est l'essentiel. [49]

Henri has "experienced" the military life (aventures), life with Lucile (l'amour), and the professional life (les études). He has strayed from the "maison du père" against his father's wishes, but is now back in the "chambre du père," only with Berne in the father's "peignoir de bain blanc." Mathile, who has represented completely passive acceptance throughout the play, then establishes the sum total of his actions. "Tout est comme avant." [50] Fruitless repetition of meaningless action has only intensified Henri's anguish at his own weakness. Nothing has changed, for he has failed to really act. He screams, "Assez!," [51] and kills Berne, the first viable act of revolt in Adamov's theater, the first successful attempt to break out of the nightmare of emptiness. *Le Sens de la Marche* is, as Jean Duvignaud suggests, a play of infinite suffering and ultimate revolt.

> *Le Sens de la Marche,* cette histoire d'un homme qui tente de s'arracher à ce qu'il est, de parvenir à cette plénitude où la vie ne fait qu'un avec la tendresse. Comme dans tout ce qu'écrit Adamov, dont le talent me paraît plus vigoureux sinon plus dense que celui de Samuel Beckett, nous retrouvons un art lucide du dialogue et du geste, une indiscutable grandeur pathétique. Le héros du *Sens de la Marche* approfondit en lui-même, comme le suggère Georges Bataille, "le supplice" d'une souffrance infinie. [52]

The paralysis of the will, the absence of meaningful action that dominates *Le Sens de la Marche* is also characteristic of *Tous contre tous,* the last of the "police-state" plays. Jean Rist, the protagonist of the play, like Henri, experiences a life controlled by others — his mother, Marie his wife, Zenno the man he originally befriends, the State. Only at the very end of the play and then with the inspiration of his beloved Noémie does he dare to revolt. It is a first act directed

---

[49] *Le Sens de la Marche,* p. 62.
[50] *Le Sens de la Marche,* p. 63.
[51] *Le Sens de la Marche,* p. 64.
[52] Jean Duvignaud, "Le Théâtre: la promesse," *Nouvelle Nouvelle Revue Française,* No. 3 (mars, 1953), pp. 520-21.

against the emptiness of his life, much like that of Henri. But whereas Henri commits murder by strangling Berne, Jean accepts death nobly at the hands of the totalitarian State in order to achieve an identity on the metaphysical level.

Like *La grande et la petite manœuvre*, *Tous contre tous* blends cohesively the exterior drama of political persecution with the interior drama of existential anguish. As Geneviève Serreau indicates in her *Histoire du "nouveau théâtre,"* the two levels coexist.

> Dans *Tous contre tous* ... la persécution des Juifs (les "Réfugiés") forme la structure extérieure du drame, mais elle est dominée par une autre torture plus terrifiante, avec toutes ses implications métaphysiques: la torture de vivre qui travaillait déjà les héros de *La Parodie*. Les deux motifs cœxistent et on ne peut nier qu'ils se gênent mutuellement. [53]

But as a play it is significantly more specific in its terms than *La grande et la petite manœuvre* or the other "police-state" plays. Persecution on the political level, while still not represented as that of a particular state in historical time, is clearly defined in this play as an attack against a particular group, the "réfugiés," those who are marked by their limping. The limping is, of course, Adamov's attempt to translate literally and concretely the attitude of others, of the majority towards a specific group of minority. One need not see the "réfugiés" as Jews, but rather as any persecuted minority. They "limp" because they are "marked," the limping is a "sign" and a result of prejudice and those who limp are those who accept the judgement or prejudice of others. But the play does move significantly away from political oppression as an abstract in the direction of specific oppression of specific peoples.

Tous contre tous is also richer in texture, more complex in detail than the other "police-state" plays. This results principally from the fact that the protagonist Jean experiences on the political level both the fear of the "réfugiés" and the power of the State. He is both victim and persecutor depending on the vagaries of his political fortunes. But while his relationship to the State fluctuates, his inner drama remains constant as Jean Rist himself admits.

---

[53] Serreau, p. 73.

> On est comme on est, on n'y peut rien. Et les choses aussi,
> elles sont comme elles sont. [54]

It is the posture of passive acceptance so familiar in the early plays
of Adamov. Only the love for and the example of his beloved Noémie,
a refugee who does not limp, convince Jean that he can no longer
live in fear, that he must act as a free agent.

> On ne peut pas vivre continuellement dans la peur, ce n'est
> pas possible, ça se venge à la fin. [55]

Only then does Jean resist the debilitating voices — his mother, Zenno
and the State — and escape from the confinement of his psychological
impotency to die courageously. Unlike the Mutilé of *La grande et la
petite manœuvre* who could not break the hypnotic spell of the "Voix
des moniteurs" by his love and faith in Erna, Jean finds strength in
Noémie and makes a leap to freedom and death.

The two dramas, interior and exterior, mesh so perfectly in this
play that it is only by apparent defeat on the political level that Jean
achieves a sort of victory on the metaphysical level. The sixteen
tableaux of *Tous contre tous* are divided into two parts. During the
ten tableaux of the Première Partie the "réfugiés" are progressively
more and more persecuted. Jean, a non-refugee, befriends the limping
Zenno in the opening scene of the play, but his attitude towards the
minority hardens into fullfledged persecution when he loses his wife
Marie to the very man he had saved. When the fortune of the refugees
temporarily changes in their favor in the Deuxième Partie, Jean is
in turn sought as an enemy of the State for his former excess of zeal
in the racial persecution. A victim of the State, he flees with his
mother in the disguise of a "boiteux," meets Noémie, a non-limping
refugee, and falls in love with her. When once again the State begins
to persecute the refugees, he is faced with the choice of dying nobly
as a refugee with his beloved Noémie or seeking escape as Jean Rist,
"l'agitateur de village."

Yet the real conflict of the play is not between minority and
majority groups, but between those who limp, Zenno and La Mère,
and those who don't, Jean and Noémie, between those who live in

---

[54] Arthur Adamov, *Tous contre tous* in *Théâtre I* (Paris, 1953), p. 150.
[55] *Tous contre tous*, p. 196.

fear and those who reject life on others' terms. Thus the metaphysical
drama crosses the boundary lines of political, social and economic
distinction. It is the drama of Jean who, while not a refugee, chooses
to limp in order to live, a man who trembles in the presence of his
mother, a man suspicious of his wife, lacking in courage, conviction
and confidence.

> J'attendrai des heures, tout le monde passera, mais moi, on
> me passera en arrière. Moi, on ne me verra pas. Les autres,
> on les voit, on les écoute, pas moi. [56]

He is willing to limp, i.e., to lower himself in the eyes of others, to
escape the responsibility of his actions, actions precipitated by his hate
of Zenno for the seduction of his wife. All of his acts and attitudes
are directed by fear, fear of his mother, fear of Zenno, fear of the
State. Only at the very end of the play does he choose to be free
and accept death as the consequence of his action. Only the example
of Noémie is capable of sustaining his thrust out of the confining
hell of others towards freedom. She is a marked person, but within
the framework of this play, she is the way to being. She is, as Renée
Saurel indicates, a refugee who refuses hate and fear.

> C'est une réfugiée. Mais elle ne boite pas. On voit sur son
> visage lisse et pur qu'elle mourra peut-être mais qu'elle ne
> boitera jamais, que la haine, la peur, la persécution ne feront
> jamais d'elle ce qu'elles ont fait d'un Zenno. [57]

Thus while all four principals — La Mère, Zenno, Noémie and
Jean — die as political victims at the end of the play, Jean dies will-
ingly, meaningfully. His death is an act of revolt against a system
which is in reality only an extension of the psychological impotency
of the individuals making up the system. For the play implies, as
George E. Wellwarth points out in *The Theater of Protest and
Paradox,* that the repressive social system results from the personal
selfishness of the people making up the society.

> *Tous contre tous* is undoubtedly Adamov's best play . . . the
> play is not so much an indictment of a social system which

---

[56] *Tous contre tous*, p. 151.

[57] Renée Saurel, "*Tous contre tous* d'Arthur Adamov," *Les Temps modernes,* No. 91 (juin, 1953), p. 2033.

forces human beings to act in their habitual dog-eat-dog manner as an implication that the social system is a result of human nature: a social system, Adamov is saying, is no more than a conglomeration of individuals and their traits. The only rule the individual respects is the rule of self; therefore, the society in which he lives is an impersonal one where the law of self-preservation is the only guiding principle and treachery the accepted mode of conduct. [58]

Jean, his resistance fortified by his love for Noémie, rejects the system and thereby rejects his former self. We are left with a vague hope that on certain levels the political oppression of "tous contre tous" can reveal to us the interior oppression of the human condition, that as Jean Duvignaud suggests, persecution is self-revelatory.

> Adamov paraît demander à la persécution qui tourmente ses héros ce que les peuples archaïques demandent à la peur: révéler à l'homme ce qui le dégrade. [59]

What degrades Jean, what robs him of real human action as the play opens, is intensified by a series of situations wherein he is continually revealed to himself as psychologically impotent. The progressively intertwining plots of exterior and interior disorder of the play coalesce into a moment of paroxysm pushing him towards the brink of ultimate choice. The original absence of a notion of self free of others is intensified by the degradation that it entails leading to a progressive disintegration of the play's universe. Significantly in this play the hero, redeemed by the saving grace of Woman, refuses further degradation and chooses death as a positive value.

Modern man, in the plays of Adamov, is radically alone, a victim of self (his lost spiritual dimension) and a victim of others, of the State ("les puissances sont incarnées par des hommes"), for the mysterious powers of the human condition that crush him are mediated by man in society. In this sense he is truly "tragic," separated, as Lucien Goldmann points out, from both God and man.

> C'est dire que, situé à égale distance de Dieu et du monde le héros tragique est *radicalement seul,* à tel point que le

---

[58] George E. Wellwarth, *The Theater of Protest and Paradox* (New York, 1964), pp. 29-30.

[59] Duvignaud, "Le Théâtre d'Adamov," p. 730.

> véritable problème de la tragédie est celui de savoir comment . . . il peut encore y avoir dialogue. [60]

He is persecuted from within and from without. The "dialogue" he once held with God and fellow man is but a vague memory. Adamov's four "police-state"plays express in very real terms this isolation, concretize this alienation of man in poetic images that recognize the inefficacy of words alone and the uselessness of traditional psychology. It is the reality of the persecution, of the destruction of man from within and from without that is literally portrayed on the stage. And as Adamov insists in *Auguste Strindberg, Dramaturge,* the play must demonstrate the fact of persecution and not just talk about it.

> Mais comment prouver la réalité de la persécution dont il est l'objet? En racontant les faits? Mais les paroles isolées n'ont pas de poids. Ce qu'il faut, c'est *montrer* les faits. [61]

---

[60] Lucien Goldmann, *Jean Racine, Dramaturge* (Paris, 1956), pp. 25-26.
[61] *Strindberg,* p. 53.

CHAPTER III

A PERIOD OF SYNTHESIS

Le Ping-Pong and *Paolo Paoli* mark a significant period in Adamov's theater. By the mid 1950's the playwright had established himself as an important force in the "new theater" in France. His first eight plays had demonstrated a dramaturgy that exhibited many of the techniques of the then current avant-garde while also revealing a world vision which shared much in common with what has come to be called the Theater of the Absurd.

Le Ping-Pong of 1955 seemed at the time to many critics to be a significant break-through, an obvious development and shift in direction. Adamov himself shared this view, for as he wrote in the *Note préliminaire* to *Théâtre II*:

> Contrairement à ce qui se passe dans mes autres pièces, de *La Parodie* aux *Retrouvailles*, la menace ne vient pas que du dehors; les personnages secrètent leur propre poison, préparent leur propre malheur; et ce malheur, n'ayant pas exactement les mêmes causes pour chacun, n'a pas du tout les mêmes resultats. [1]

Having begun to write the play with only the closing image of two old men playing ping-pong, Adamov felt free to allow his characters to create situations. Moreover, the play was situated in a relatively specific time and place by virtue of the very images themselves, for example, the pinball machine.

---

[1] Arthur Adamov, *Note préliminaire* in *Théâtre II* (Paris, 1955), pp. 16-17.

Paolo Paoli (1957) examined a particular society based on the profit motive as well as the destructive forces unleased by such a society, forces leading to a World War. It was then judged by many critics as marking Adamov's abandonment of his previous vision and style, a play, according to Martin Esslin, which divorced itself and its author from his early work and the tradition of the avant-garde Theater of the Absurd.

> It (*Paolo Paoli*) marks Adamov's abandonment of the Theater of the Absurd and his adherence to another equally significant movement of the modern stage — the Brechtian "epic theater." [2]

But it would seem on closer investigation and in light of subsequent developments that the two plays, while central to the theater of Adamov in time and significance, merely mark a new variation of the basic pattern which informs his theater. The traditional notion of *Le Ping-Pong* as a transition play and *Paolo Paoli* as the first of a new type of "realistic" committed theater yields on closer analysis to the recognition that the two plays are vertical constituents of the same horizontal process which makes up the total theater of Adamov.

Thus we see this particular unit of *Le Ping-Pong* and *Paolo Paoli* as amplification rather than reorientation, development rather than change, growth rather than rebirth. The two plays reveal the same basic repetitive structure of intensification characteristic of the earlier plays. Moreover, man is still a victim, separated from others as he is separated from a lost spiritual or unifying dimension. He is a prisoner of himself and others; the political and social condition of which he is victim is but an extension of his psychological and spiritual emptiness. Proportions and degrees vary from play to play, but the same basic themes of absence of authentic values, of guilt, of the impossibility of communication, of inner and exterior ignominy persist. The world of *Le Ping-Pong* and *Paolo Paoli* is ultimately the same seemingly absurd universe of the early plays, but within a more specific and pronounced exterior conflict.

From *La Parodie* to *Si l'été revenait* man, in the theater of Adamov, is always victim and oppressor, both of himself and others.

---

[2] Martin Esslin, *The Theatre of the Absurd* (New York, 1961), p. 69.

Incapable of inner harmony, he creates exterior chaos. A prisoner of his own neuroses, of his own personal ignominy, he projects an ignominious society. There is no escape from himself (the inner dilemma) and no escape from others (the exterior dilemma). While the accent shifts from play to play, the dual dilemma persists.

Le Ping-Pong, in many ways Adamov's most successful play, is perhaps the best synthesis of this dual dilemma, located, as Geneviève Serreau points out, at a privileged point of intersection:

> A la croisée des chemins, *Le Ping-Pong* semble bien être son chef-d'œuvre, la pièce où des contradictions non encore résolues s'affrontent et s'incarnent avec le maximum de fermeté, d'humour, de sens du mystère, par une maîtrise originale du langage scénique. [3]

The two principal characters, Arthur and Victor, suffer from both their own defects as well as the shortcomings of the society in which they live. Moreover, we come to see that it is their very defects which create or permit to continue that very society of which they are victims.

Two young men, Arthur, an art student, and Victor, a student of medicine, are fascinated by the pinball machine. It has become central in their life, a means whereby to pass time, to avoid the responsibility of classes, to impress the young Annette, to dream and create by. They soon discover by way of Sutter, a representative of the Consortium, that the machine can be more than just a game, that it can lead to financial security and social prestige. All their energeies are then directed toward gaining entrance into the power structure which is the Consortium. Soon the pinball and all that it stands for dominates their entire existence. They are continually seeking to modify the machine by new ideas which will bring them financial reward and social acceptance. Some of their "inventions" are accepted by Le Vieux, the director of the Consortium, and some are rejected. Scenes change from a café to a bathhouse to a shoe store to a dance hall, but it is always the pinball machine — or its absence — which dominates the scene and the dialogue.

Midway through the play, when one of their ideas is rejected, Victor abandons Arthur and the Consortium to finish his medical

---

[3] Geneviève Serreau, *Histoire du "nouveau théâtre"* (Paris, 1966), p. 82.

studies. Arthur continues alone making the pinball his life's work. Time passes and fortunes change. Le Vieux dies, Annette is killed. In the final scene Victor and Arthur are once again reunited, this time as two old men playing ping-pong together just as seriously and comically as they had once played the pinball machine. Victor collapses and apparently dies of a heart attack. Seized with panic, Arthur, now alone and totally meaningless, vainly cries out his name.

The twelve tableaux in two parts of *Le Ping-Pong* which cover the life span of the two protagonists from youth to old age reveal a rich texture with a wide assortment of defined characters — Arthur and Victor, Annette, Sutter, Roger, Mme Duranty, Le Vieux — as well as a complex set of relationships — Arthur-Victor, Annette-Roger-Sutter, Annette-Arthur-Victor, Arthur-Victor-Le Vieux. Moreover, the drama of these personal relationships is played out against the larger canvas of social and political change indicated by the rise and fall of the Consortium in its battle against the "stands" and their nationalization. But sustaining the rich texture of *Le Ping-Pong* is the same basic unifying pattern of the earlier more schematic plays. The opening image of the play, Arthur and Victor as young men squabbling over the machine as they play at pinball, is repeated by variation throughout the entire play reaching its most intense statement in the closing image of two old men playing ping-pong without a net or rackets, Victor's death, and the ultimate loneliness of Arthur. Following different paths, life had brought them back to the same starting point only intensified by age and their past experiences. The differences in their character, the varying roles they played in life, are obviated by the final triumphant image of futility wherein they are reduced to almost identical fates.

Beginning as pinball enthusiasts in the opening scene, they had worked more or less together as professional consultants to the Consortium throughout the Première Partie. Then when Victor abandoned the Consortium, Arthur pursued fame and fortune in the pinball dynasty alone throughout the Deuxième Partie. But the final scene reduces their different efforts to basically the same fate. This closing image is all the more ironic when we recall Arthur talking to Victor in the opening scene.

Et moi, tu voudrais que, pendant ce temps, je prépare ma licence. Eh bien non, je ne la préparerai pas, car, à tout prendre, j'aime encore mieux corriger des copies que de perdre ma jeunesse pour, à soixante-dix-sept ans, faire, tous les dimanches après-midi une partie de billard avec un collègue du même âge. [4]

While there is a degree of freedom permitted the characters of *Le Ping-Pong* which had been absent in the earlier plays, ultimately this freedom is revealed as illusory. Like N. and the Employé before them, Arthur and Victor are substantially victims of their own illusions and the illusions of the profit-oriented society in which they live. The rich texture of *Le Ping-Pong* is an elaboration and amplification of the statement concerning the futility of all human endeavor that characterizes Adamov's work. The two young "lost souls" playing the pinball in the opening scene have become, no matter what they do, the two old "lost souls playing ping-pong in the closing scene. The play's structure is an intensification by repetition with variation of the meaninglessness of their existence. Death, the final futility of life, overtakes Victor and exposes Arthur to the truth of his situation.

Much of the humor and pathos of *Le Ping-Pong* revolves around the central object of the play, the pinball machine. More accurately, it results from the distance between the grandiose effort, constant concern, flights of poetry and persistent energy of the principal characters and the relative triviality of the object of their dedication. Though trivial and even frivolous, the pinball machine, as Geneviève Serreau suggests, represents in the play a certain type of profit-oriented society:

> Une image-force est à l'origine du *Ping-Pong*: celle, dérisoire, de deux vieillards en train d'échanger des balles de ping-pong. Un objet-force (si l'on peut dire) la domine: le billard électrique, qui représente plus qu'il ne symbolise une certaine société d'argent et les prestiges truqués dont elle se pare. C'est autour de cet immuable personnage-objet que s'organisent-ou plutôt s'enchevêtrent-les péripéties d'une action très complexe. [5]

The machine, at first a diversion, becomes a means to an end and finally an end in itself. Victor and especially Arthur give themselves

[4] Arthur Adamov, *Le Ping-Pong* in *Théâtre II* (Paris, 1955), p. 111.
[5] Serreau, p. 75.

so totally to the machine that they become guilty of making of it
something other than what it is. Society, or more specifically profit-
based society, shares in the guilt, for the Consortium shows them how
the machine can procure a meaning in life for them. They learn to
live by it, seek social acceptance by it, use it as a poetic stimulus,
create illusions by it and seek power by it. Ultimately they are responsible for wasting their lives in the worship of false gods, for attempting to find happiness and meaning outside of themselves, for
evading the essential dilemma of their human condition. Their instinct
to create, their capacity for love, their need to share with others in
a viable community are perverted and athrophied. It is a parody of
life and not life itself that they live. Rather it is a life similar to that
of the machine itself once it has tilted, the ball rolling past the
bumpers and flippers meaninglessly, the soul gone from the game.
Arthur, in the opening scene, fixedly watches the machine which he
has just tilted.

> Et la bille continue de rouler, naturellement, alors que ça
> ne sert plus à rien, que rien ne s'allume, que tout est bloqué.
> Regarde! [6]

The vitality of their youth, the spiritual and mental growth of
their manhood have been blocked by the overly preponderant role
of the pinball in their lives. Martin Esslin in *The Theatre of the
Absurd* speaks of the machine as an ambiguous symbol:

> The pinball machine has all the fascinating ambiguity of a
> symbol. It may stand for capitalism and big business, but it
> may equally stand for any religious or political ideology that
> secretes its own organization and apparatus of power, that de-
> mands devotion and loyalty from its adherents. [7]

But while the machine may have "all the fascinating ambiguity of a
symbol," it is foremost a literal image central to the play, a concrete
object which dominates the protagonists' existence, corrupts their
vision, informs their language, and invalidates their energies. Roland
Barthes in his *Mythologies* sees it as an agent producing dramatic
situations:

---

[6] *Le Ping-Pong*, p. 112.
[7] Esslin, p. 68.

> Or le billard électrique du *Ping-Pong* ne symbolise rien du
> tout; il n'exprime pas, il produit; c'est un objet littéral, dont
> la fonction est d'engendrer, par son objectivité même, des
> situations. [8]

And these situations are primarily situations of language. Arthur and
Annette come closest to a vital personal relationship when the two
of them wax poetic over their new idea of *fusée-lune* for the pinball
machine. Le Vieux and Arthur understand each other best when they
recognize that they both see the game of pinball as a combination of
life and death, "Mort et résurrection, le tout pour dix francs!" [9]
When Madame Duranty discovers Annette, whom she has known
since childhood, dead, her language betrays her priorities.

> Devant le stand! Il fallait que je la trouve ... dans cet état,
> justement devant le stand ... (Criant). Je l'ai toujours dit,
> qu'il n'y avait rien de bon à en attendre, de ces stands. [10]

It is a language which confines and compromises the principal characters. It stifles their vision, limits their field of endeavor, and leads
them still further into the labyrinth of meaningless situations and
degrading relationships.

The parody of life in *Le Ping-Pong* is the parody of language.
While ostensibly free to choose his fate, man chooses a machine as
the generator of his destiny. All his efforts, dreams, poetry, his very
soul is expended on an object meaningless in itself. But in building
his life around such a trivial object as the pinball machine, he continues to use the same language and thereby degrades it. And this, as
Adamov says in *L'Aveu*, is the most telling sign of man's fall from
grace:

> La dégradation du langage est le signe visible, infaillible, du
> mal. Chaque jour, les noms que l'homme jadis proférait avec
> vénération et selon l'ordre, sont astreints aux pires contre-
> façons du sens. [11]

We live today, Adamov tells us, in a time of ignominy and the most
significant indicator of our abased state is our language:

---

[8] Roland Barthes, *Mythologies* (Paris, 1957), pp. 99-100.
[9] *Le Ping-Pong*, p. 116.
[10] *Le Ping-Pong*, p. 173.
[11] Arthur Adamov, *L'Aveu* (Paris, 1946), p. 108.

Et quel rapport peut-on encore établir entre ce que l'on nomme aujourd'hui hiérarchie, façade qui ne cache que le vide, morne notion fondée sur le faux prestige que confèrent la richesse et le pouvoir usurpé et la grande architecture symbolique de l'ancienne hiérarchie sacrée? [12]

The apparent freedom or liberty of the principal characters in *Le Ping-Pong* must be weighed against the limitations of choice created by a society based on the profit motive. The power of the Consortium to persuade Arthur and others that reality is the perfecting of the pinball machine, that fulfillment rests in the rearrangement of bumpers and flippers, that their dreams of romance and success can be realized by devotion to a game is the power of modern capitalistic society to rob them of the very freedoms it promises. The feelings of persecution, inferiority, and insecurity, the inordinate need for diversion and social acceptance which characterize man's lost unifying dimension, his loss of "la grande architecture symbolique de l'ancienne hiérarchie sacrée," are the very defects which permit such a society as this to exist, which permit the Consortium, or any agency like it, to grow by feeding on their needs and vanity, by incorporating them as active members in the very process which robs them of their vitality, choice, and meaningfulness.

But the society can be guilty, the play shows us, only to the degree that its constituents permit it. Roger, who has never hesitated to disparage the pinball as a type of distraction, does not hesitate in the least to reap the fruits of its attraction for and domination of others by becoming secretary to Le Vieux.

C'est vrai, Monsieur Constantin, je n'aime pas travailler, mais j'admets très bien que les autres travaillent. [13]

Jealousy, vanity, greed, fear — these individual syndromes — permit the societal diseases which in turn feed on the individual. Thus Adamovian man is both oppressor and oppressed, victim and persecutor. The amplification which characterizes *Le Ping-Pong* as well as *Paolo Paoli* and makes of these two plays a new unit is that the parody of life posited in Adamov's first play *La Parodie* is described

---

[12] *L'Aveu,* p. 109.
[13] *Le Ping-Pong,* p. 119.

in this play as it develops. The specificity of context — the pinball industry in a modern city within a capitalistic society — is the necessary element which permits us to view the how and why of man's situation. The situation itself — man helpless in a hostile universe — has remained constant. Moreover, the "how" and "why" which lead to man's parody of life in this play can and will change in other plays, that is, the mechanisms which pull the puppet's strings will vary from play to play. But the essential dilemma, the situation of man spiritually bankrupt and prey to the vices of the world in which he lives and creates is constant throughout Adamov's entire work.

The achievement of *Le Ping-Pong, Paolo Paoli,* and most of the later plays is that they show us how individual man himself, while unavoidably a victim of the existing political and social order, is also ultimately responsible for it. In that sense Adamov is correct in stating that in this play,

> La menace ne vient pas que du dehors; les personnages secrètent leur propre poison, préparent leur propre malheur; [14]

But as we have seen, this is also true, if to a lesser degree and less specifically, of the early plays. It is man's loss of a spiritual and unifying dimension which propels him out of fear and feelings of insufficiency and guilt, to create or to perpetuate an oppressive external order. Thus when Victor dies at the end of the play and Arthur calls out his name, we are left with the beautiful unresolved ambiguity of knowing who is the "victor," Victor who dies and escapes, or Arthur who lives on, but who is now old and alone, robbed of the one meaningful factor in his life, his friendship with Victor.

Both Victor and Arthur ultimately know despair, frustration and defeat in the pursuit of power and prestige to fill the void of their existence. The promise of a new beginning — the machine, the Consortium, Annette — is still the illusion that the Employé chases in *La Parodie.* And like Lili, the eternal woman around whom man gravitates, she who offers both hope and despair, salvation and castration, Annette is a promise unfulfilled, not only to Arthur and Victor, but also to Roger, Sutter, and even Le Vieux.

---

[14] *Note préliminaire* in *Théâtre II,* pp. 16-17.

Le Ping-Pong is a play, moreover, which demands even more skilled staging than most of Adamov's other plays. The full meaning of the text can only be effected by a judicious balance between the literal images with which the play abounds and the language to which they give birth. The anger, frustration, joy, hope, despair, and poetic flights of the principal characters must be played off against the dominating and central image of the pinball machine in order that the emptiness of their lives be fully felt in all its dimensions. Only by such a utilization of the text does the play achieve its full realization of its theatrical space that Artaud demanded in his *Le Théâtre et son double*:

> Les images et les mouvements employés ne seront là seulement pour le plaisir extérieur des yeux ou de l'oreille, mais pour celui plus secret et plus profitable de l'esprit. Ainsi l'espace théâtral sera utilisé, non seulement dans ses dimensions et dans son volume, mais, si l'on peut dire, *dans ses dessous.* [15]

Paolo Paoli, like the early plays, is primarily concerned with the eternal questions of man's fate in an incomprehensible universe. But like its immediate predecessor *Le Ping-Pong* it places these questions in a specific context of place and especially time, the 20th century, what Adamov in *L'Aveu* has called *le temps de l'ignominie*. This specificity of context as defined in *Le Ping-Pong* and *Paolo Paoli* is an added yet integral element of most of the plays written since 1955, an element which further places Adamov in what Geneviève Serreau has described as the mainstream of significant post-war theater in France:

> En somme, nous voici ramenés brutalement à quelques questions essentielles, celles-là même qui d'Eschyle à Shakespeare, à Calderon et à Kleist (pour ne citer que quelques noms) traversent les siècles et les scènes de théâtre du monde entier. L'important est qu'elles soient posées, non dans le vide, mais dans le tumulte concret d'une époque, non sous une forme éternelle, mais solidement, dans le terreau éphémère où notre histoire s'enracine. [16]

---

[15] Antonin Artaud, *Le Théâtre et son double* (Paris, 1964), p. 188.
[16] Serreau, p. 25.

Moreover, this added dimension of specificity of context facilitates the developing shift of emphasis in Adamov's work from what he has called "le mal incurable des choses" to the "mal curable," from the inner to the exterior dilemma, from the evil apparently inherent in man's human condition to the evil created and perpetuated by man himself in society. *Paolo Paoli* is in a very real sense a variation on *Le Ping-Pong*, a further development of the apparent contradiction that man is his own victim, that the political and social condition to which he is subject and by which he is victimized is but an extension of his own psychical and spiritual malady. *Paolo Paoli* moves further in the direction of explanation first manifested in *Le Ping-Pong*. For while the early plays make the statement of man's position as victim, the transitional plays demonstrate in varying degrees the machinery of exploitation, isolation, alienation, suffering, greed, fear, etc. that make man a victim of himself and others. Moreover, the transitional plays become richer in texture because they seek to explain the very processes themselves. In speaking of Paolo Paoli while the play was still in progress, Adamov said in the *Note préliminaire* to *Théâtre II*:

> Si déjà j'entrais dans la "machine à sous," et il me fallait y entrer, je devais essayer d'examiner les rouages de la grande machine aussi assidûment que j'examinais bumpers et flippers. Cet examen, j'essaie aujourd'hui de le faire dans une nouvelle pièce, plus située encore en un temps et un milieu que *Le Ping-Pong*. [17]

This "new" play, *Paolo Paoli*, while further situated in a time and a milieu and while more complex in plot than *Le Ping-Pong*, is a masterpiece of condensation. It is a play which suggests the entire gamut of political, social, religious, national and especially spiritual forces leading to World War I while demonstrating at the same time the relationship between societal and personal concerns, the dual dilemma of man's condition. Its twelve tableaux, divided into two equal parts, span the period of la *belle époque*, 1900-1914, as experienced by only seven characters, and yet these seven serve to represent a significant cross-section of the society in which they live and the social forces which propel this society towards its own destruction.

---

[17] *Note préliminaire* in *Théâtre II*, p. 17.

Paolo Paoli is at the center of the play's universe, the central force of a galaxy of convicts, priests, industrialists, chauvinists, social activists, shop owners and kept women. As the play opens he is a dealer in rare butterflies, an apparently frivolous commodity, but we quickly see in the opening tableau how society in terms of the exploiters and the exploited relates to him, how he is both the cause and effect of societal degradation. A partial explanation for his success in this exotic industry lies in his source of butterflies, the cheap slave labor of convicts in the French penal colony of Guyane, a source resulting from his father's governmental position as overseer. Paolo supplies these butterflies to clients such a Hulot-Vasseur, a manufacturer and importer of ostrich feathers and an anticlerical nationalist. But because this wealthy collector is interested in certain Chinese specimens, Paolo manages to enlist the help of the Abbé Saulnier and the Chinese converts of his missionary brother Basile. And because Paolo's "half-German, half-protestant" wife Stella is interested in opening her own "petit salon de modes," Paolo convinces the successful Hulot-Vasseur to supply her at favorable prices with the necessary feathers and thereby make her his client. Meanwhile Stella's servant Rose awaits the return of her husband Robert Marpeaux, a convict-supplier of butterflies, who has escaped the penal colony and is now at large in Venezuela.

Thus the opening tableau quickly establishes the terms of the play, the total fabric of the society with its intense interrelationships. The small businessman Paolo lives by supplying butterflies to the bigger industrialist Hulot-Vasseur who lives by the feather industry which permits him to aid Stella in opening her own fashion shop. The needs of the anti-clerical free-thinker are satisfied by a priest using religion in the form of Chinese converts. The servant Rose is reduced to dependence on these very people because of the machinery of their society which had unjustly imprisoned her husband with the result that she in turn is forced to support and help perpetuate that very society. It is a fabric of self-interest and self-justification wherein profit substitutes for principle, expediency for good, the material for the spiritual, a society whose *Leitmotif* might well be Paolo's restatement in the opening scene of the Pascalian maxim:

> La raison a ses raisons que le cœur lui-même ne connaît
> pas. [18]

This pattern of each man using the other to his personal advantage
repeats itself continually with slight modifications throughout the entire play, growing in intensity and seriousness of effect as the war
grows closer. Stella uses Rose the servant, Paolo the husband, Hulot
the lover and business associate, and finally France and Germany to
her own selfish ends and is in turn rejected by them all. The Abbé
Saulnier betrays his friend Paolo when it is to his advantage to do
business with the anti-clerical Hulot-Vasseur. Later he sacrifices Robert
to protect these same advantages, justifying his action with "religious"
rationalizations.

Hulot-Vasseur is less hypocritical in avowing his motivations than
the Abbé. He is the determined businessman ready to process whatever
product the public demands. If war will further his ends, then chauvinistic militarism is a virtue. He is a barometer of social, economic
and political fortunes ready to sacrifice ostrich feathers for his country's needs, prepared to forsake the "good life" of *la belle époque* for
the police-state of war. Robert, the ardent anti-militaristic socialist,
explains Hulot-Vasseur to his wife Rose:

> Mais, petite bécasse, si Hulot s'est mis aux boutons d'uni-
> forme, ça veut dire qu'après la guerre des Balkans, qui a
> permis à ces messieurs d'essayer leur matériel, il va y avoir
> la vraie guerre, partout, si on ne fait rien pour l'empêcher. [19]

Hulot uses Robert as he uses everyone he can, the Abbé, Stella, and
even Paolo. When it is to his convenience, he hires Robert, the progressive unionist, to train the Abbé's Catholic "jaunes." But as he
betrays his country for reasons of greed, so he betrays this same Robert
for leading the C.G.T. boycott against his factory.

But it is Robert Marpeaux and his wife Rose who are most exploited by the people with whom they come into contact, by the political and economic forces of the society which dominates them. As
a prisoner in Guyane, Robert works diligently for Paolo as his wife
Rose serves Stella. When he escapes, returns to France and wants his

---

[18] Arthur Adamov, *Paolo Paoli* (Paris, 1957), p. 22.
[19] *Paolo Paoli*, p. 246.

case reopened, Paolo "helps" him by sending him off to a war-town Morocco to collect butterflies. It soon becomes apparent that in this world man and not butterflies or ostrich feathers is the real commodity. For Paolo, Robert's survival can be purchased by chasing butterflies. For the Abbé, Robert's redemption will be bought as a soldier in his country's army. For Hulot, his worth is in training and organizing workers for the buttons of this army's uniforms. Robert is seen not as a human being with a wife and a life to be lived freely but as a commodity to be bought and sold, a figure to be shifted from role to role within the society.

But when Marpeaux is arrested, denounced by the Abbé at Hulot's instigation, it is Paolo who comes to his aid, who forces the sale of the famous Charaxes butterfly on the Abbé in order to pay for Robert's release:

> Je vous (l'Abbé) retiens parce que j'ai changé d'avis, et que je vais vous vendre mon Charaxes. Il faut bien que j'aide un peu Rose et Robert qui, par votre faute, et un peu par la mienne, je le reconnais. . . . [20]

It is an action born of guilt, frustration, despair and spite. Paolo sees himself as one of the many, as part of the fabric of the exploiting and degrading society which has caused such harm to the couple, which is responsible for Robert's anger and attacks against the capitalist system as well as Rose's betrayal of her husband for the more affluent and influential Paolo. He says to Rose:

> Prends-le, nigaude! Tu as honte? Pourquoi? De l'argent, on vous en doit, à vous deux, Hulot-Vasseur, moi, les autres; on vous en doit même plus que ça, pour toutes les heures qu'on vous a volées. [21]

Paolo's action is a revolt against a system of which he is part, a debilitating and demeaning circular network of interwoven self-interest and self-perpetuation. He lashes out to thwart a machinery which he now recognizes to be not only destructive of others, of the people, of the Roses and Roberts, but even of the very forces which manipulate the machinery:

---

[20] *Paolo Paoli,* p. 283.
[21] *Paolo Paoli,* p. 285.

> Mais sachez, sachez bien, mon petit Saulnier, que cet argent-là, vous pouvez lui dire adieu. Que cet argent-là ne reviendra plus tourner dans le sale petit circuit! Que cet argent-là, le quelqu'un et la quelqu'une qui vont en disposer ne le refileront pas à quelqu'un pour en soutirer quelque chose, qu'ils refileront encore à quelqu'un qui refilera encore ce quelque chose à quelqu'un pour ... et cætera ... Cet argent-là, il ira tout droit à ceux qui en ont besoin pour manger, s'habiller, et vous embêter, ce qui revient au même ... [22]

That his act is a politically and economically naive gesture of defiance against the "grande machine" is not the point. The act is Paolo's purgation and absolution, his momentary victory over self and system, his personal triumph and salvation.

In a play in which all are victims and oppressors in varying degrees, the specific drama of exploitation of which Robert and Rose are merely the most explicit symbols is repeated with increasing intensity and minor variation until it is gradually seen to be part of the larger drama of the social and political conflicts which ultimately lead to a world war. The opening image of the play — the exotic butterfly as central to the relationship Paolo-Abbé-Hulot-Robert, as linking the exploitation of a convict to the Church and French industry — is repeated by variation throughout the play reaching its most intense point in the closing image, Paolo selling the Charaxes to Hulot's intermediary the Abbé in order to save Robert. It is the most intense variation of the central image because of its apparent change (Paolo seeks to break the "sale circuit") but ultimate similarity (the gesture is economically naive and politically inept). Adamov himself stresses the importance of repetition to the play in *Ici et Maintenant*:

> Cette répétition, ce piétinement des situations — dans la première partie et même au début de la deuxième-je l'ai voulu. Non comme un principe général de théâtre (encore que je l'aie souvent employé dans mes anciennes pièces), mais particulièrement dans *Paolo Paoli*. [23]

The events, images and exploitations of the *Première Partie*, 1900-1906, parallel but with increasing intensity and seriousness of conse-

---

[22] *Paolo Paoli*, pp. 286-87.

[23] Arthur Adamov, *Ici et maintenant* (Paris, 1964), p. 86.

quence the events, images and exploitations of the *Deuxième Partie*, 1912-1914. Thus the Paolo who deals in butterflies and penal colonies in the *Première Partie* deals in butterfly objects of a nationalist and religious motif in the *Deuxième Partie*. The Hulot-Vasseur who gained his fortune at the expense of others' labor in the ostrich feather industry of the *Première Partie* increases his fortune at the expense of their labor and lives in the button industry which will furnish uniforms to the nation's army. The objects seem to change, but it is this very change which intensifies the basic similarity of the real commodity on which the system is based. And that commodity is, of course, man; for the real product is the sale of human time and flesh which remains constant throughout the play. Robert, and to a lesser extent, Rose are exploited by Paolo, the Abbé, Hulot, the economy, and the state. The events of the times of which they are a part and a victim repeat themselves in growing intensity reaching the paroxysm of the First World War. The play's repetitive structure of intensification reflects a society which Adamov describes in *Ici et Maintenant* as living under the sign of repetition:

> C'est vrai: dans la phase historique que nous vivons, les événements se répètent, avec à chaque fois une altération minime. D'où un effet que je crois assez puissant: celui produit par le déroulement d'une certaine société qui vit effectivement sous le signe de la répétition (des mêmes erreurs, des mêmes mystifications, des mêmes ignominies). [24]

The butterflies and ostrich feathers of the *Première Partie* with their sustaining penal colony become the uniform buttons and resultant police-state of war of the closing section. The play reveals man's fate at the hands of a man-made system which exploits its components, but like its predecessor *Le Ping-Pong,* it moves further in the direction of explaining and demonstrating the machinery of this exploitation. In doing this it coincides with Adamov's growing concern for the correction of "le mal curable," for the remedy of those aspects of the human condition which are controlled and regulated by man in society. He maintains in *Ici et Maintenant* that:

---

[24] *Ici et Maintenant,* p. 87.

> D'une manière générale, il est toujours profitable du point de vue social, et fécond du point de vue théâtral de devoiler les ruses au moyen desquelles les classes possédantes tentent de diviser les organisations dangereuses pour elles. [25]

Yet we are never permitted in this play to lose sight of the private and personal hell to which each character is subject. There is a propitious blending of the interior dilemma of its characters within the larger canvas of social and political conflicts so aptly exposed in the play. There is the drama of Paolo losing his wife to Hulot, Robert losing his to Paolo. But especially there is the need for expiation on the part of the guilty Paolo, the need to redeem his misuse of Robert and Rose. There is always the lingering presence of a human drama below and beyond the political and social level, the very human need to communicate, the thrust to establish human relations, to break through the barriers of political, social and economic concerns to a deeper, more human, more spiritual dimension. It is this level to which Rose appeals when she cries out to Robert:

> Ecoute, Robert, je suis trop fatiguée pour m'occuper... de généralités. Si je suis venue, c'est.... c'est parce que je n'en pouvais plus, parce que j'avais besoin de parler à... un ami, qui me comprendrait, me conseillerait... Et si maintenant tu te mets au-dessus de tout ça! [26]

It is to this level that Paolo aspires when he lashes out to halt the machinery of exploitation that so inhumanely crushes its victims. It is as though he would be free of the system, of the social, straitjacket that inhibits human relations, that denies man the liberty of being, that imposes a role on him rather than permit him to achieve his real identity. Society and its "civilization" has heaped layers of false identities and corrupting compromises on man. Paolo makes a first, feeble effort to strip himself and the system of its degrading and ignominious effects. In so doing he moves not only in the direction of social reform, "le mal curable," the external dilemma, but more profoundly and ultimately in the direction of personal renewal, the internal dilemma. Paolo moves in the direction Adamov assigns to man in *L'Aveu*:

---

[25] *Ici et Maintenant*, p. 41.
[26] *Paolo Paoli*, pp. 246-47.

Aujourd'hui il ne reste plus à l'homme que cette tâche:
arracher toutes les peaux mortes, se dépouiller jusqu'à se
trouver lui-même à l'heure de la grande nudité. [27]

Slowly freed of many of the personal obsessions and neurotic
nightmares central to the early plays, the theater of Adamov develops
in the transitional plays towards a synthesis of inner and exterior
dilemma, a coherent blending of the private hell of the human predicament and the "police-state" social systems which corrupt and
debase life. The personal ignominy of man's absurd posture in life
is interwoven with the political and social ignominy of the modern
epoch, what Adamov in L'Aveu called "le temps de l'ignominie," a
period wherein the hierarchy of human values is emptied of any real
meaning and has become no more than a façade for self-justification
and self-interest.

Paolo Paoli exposes man at his worst, as both victim and perpetrator of a degradation which is both personal and societal, the one
proceeding from the other. And to the extent that the play is a
successful metaphor of personal and public degradation, it reconciles
Marx and Rimbaud, what Henri Béhar in his Étude sur le théâtre
dada et surréaliste described as the goal of the surrealists:

On le sait, le projet des surréalistes consistait à concilier
Marx et Rimbaud, à changer le monde et la vie en même
temps et non successivement. [28]

Yet Paolo Paoli, like the early plays, is based on and developed
by a series of concrete images that expose rather than discuss, that
demonstrate rather than argue, that are theatrical rather than polemic.
These images are arranged in familiar repetitive patterns creating
an intense "theater language" that betrays the gradual then rapid
disintegration of the play's universe. The disproportion between the
objects of barter — the butterflies and the ostrich feathers — and the
serious language used to defend the barter grows more evident and
more revealing as the play's universe spins intensely toward the
holocaust of World War I. Moreover, the disproportion between object

---

[27] L'Aveu, p. 115.
[28] Henri Béhar, Etude sur le théâtre dada et surréaliste (Paris, 1967),
p. 314.

and language intensifies as the play reveals in circular fashion the ultimate spiritual emptiness, the lost unifying dimension of its universe which permits man to degrade himself and others while using a language of hope, progress and redemption. It is a language, Bernard Dort points out, which men use to protect themselves against reality:

> Revenons à la forme théâtrale: je veux dire au fait que ce théâtre est fondé sur le langage comme milieu humain fondamental; un langage que le spectateur doit comprendre comme un langage de protection contre l'Histoire. [29]

---

[29] Bernard Dort in Arthur Adamov, *Ici et Maintenant* (Paris, 1964), p. 83.

CHAPTER IV

THE POLITICAL PLAYS

The elusive quality of Adamov's theater is that it never seems to be what it is, but rather seems to be eternally becoming something other or more than what it is or has been. As Marc Beigbeder wrote just after the production of *Paolo Paoli* in 1957, Adamov's plays always announce another, each play is a promise of something to come:

> A vrai dire, comme il arrive quelquefois, chacune des pièces d'Adamov en annonce une autre, promet le chef-d'œuvre, la plénitude, pour le lendemain. Il n'y a pas de création sans, chez le créateur, insatisfaction. Mais il est des créateurs dont, en quelque sorte, elle est la vraie et seule création. Dont les œuvres courent pathétiquement, et avec qualité, génie, après l'œuvre-qui ne sera jamais. [1]

This explains to a large degree why there is no one play in the theater of Adamov which can stand as a prototype or basic invariant for the rest of the plays. Rather each play is a variant of the other, a restructuring and reviewing of an essentially similar yet superficially different universe. For no one play can sum up or envelop the playwright's total view; no one statement can exhaust the reality of a given subject. This was a lesson learned from the two apparently contradictory major influences on Adamov's work, the expressionist theater of Strindberg, what Adamov defined as a "jeu de fragiles surprises dans un édifice de monotonie," [2] and the epic-realist, socially committed theater of Bertolt Brecht, from which Adamov claims to

---

[1] Marc Beigbeder, *Le Théâtre en France depuis la libération* (Paris, 1959), p. 182.

[2] Arthur Adamov, *Auguste Strindberg, Dramaturge* (Paris, 1955), p. 62.

learn the peril of seeking an all enveloping formula for the expression of his duel consciousness before the havoc of human reality:

> Et j'ai même vu là une leçon, encore, que nous donne Brecht: ne pas chercher à dire dans une seule pièce tout ce qu'on a à dire, fût-ce sur un seul sujet. Rien de plus dangereux, de plus faux intellectuellement, que la recherche de la formule qui enveloppe tout, de la phrase philosophale. [3]

But it is not surprising that a lesson learned from Strindberg is relearned from Brecht, for Adamov's theater is perhaps the most effective synthesis in France of these two major contemporary traditions, a perpetually developing theater that incorporates the best elements of the two orientations. *Le Ping-Pong* and *Paolo Paoli* had marked a moment of fusion in the theater of Adamov. Rejecting some of the limitations of his early schematic plays situated in a no-man's land of eternal conflict, he had sought to concretize man's struggle within its social, political and historical context. This process of fusion or synthesis continues in the later plays with some plays accentuating the political more than the social dimension. But as Guicharnaud points out, the process is consistent and Adamov was persistent in his search for a fuller, more complete portrayal of man's condition:

> Finding the no-man's land of the plays during the 1950's too limited because it obliged the writers to go round in circles within their eternal commonplaces, Adamov wanted to give man a more complete and more concrete image, that is, to restore his social and historical dimensions by means of a synthesis of the two visions, thus achieving a total portrayal of man's condition. Obviously, his evolution consists less in repudiating past experiences than in criticizing them, in order to recover them for use on another level. [4]

It is then a matter of degree, of perspective and not change, for the theater of Adamov is continually absorbed with both the "grande" and the "petite manœuvre," man's human condition and man's social, political, and historical situation. Thus having stressed the "grande

---

[3] Arthur Adamov, *Ici et maintenant* (Paris, 1964), p. 165.

[4] Jacques Guicharnaud in collaboration with June Guicharnaud, *Modern French Theatre from Giraudoux to Genet* (New Haven and London, 1967), pp. 198-99.

manœuvre" in the early plays' Adamov's theater moves to the fore-
ground of our interest the "petite manœuvre," the "mal curable" of
man's dual dilemma. But as Martin Esslin points out, the one aspect
is never totally excluded in favor of the other:

> If in *La grande et la petite manœuvre* it was the revolution-
> aries' futile struggle that represented the small manœuvre,
> and the all-enveloping absurdity of the human condition
> dwarfing the social struggle that stood for the big manoeuvre,
> then in *Paolo Paoli* the small manoeuvre looms large and the
> large manoeuvre has receded into a barely perceptible back-
> ground. [5]

This shift in emphasis, first perceptible in *Le Ping-Pong,* more
obvious in *Paolo Paoli,* continues in the later plays, but even within
this shift there are varying emphases, various aspects of man's
situation which are predominant. However, when viewed in its totality
and in retrospect, the later orientation of Adamov's theater reveals
two basic directions or observable paradigms; (1) those plays wherein
man struggles within a primarily political context and (2) those plays
whose dimensions are essentially social.

The "political" plays, 1958-1961, represent Adamov's effort to
deal with his recognition that death, the ultimate ignominy and humiliation, does not obviate man's need to battle the historical forces
of life that would crush him. His theater exhibits a need to go beyond
the statement of life's essential "absurdity" that we find in his early
plays towards a working-out of man's political and social problems.
In speaking of his "metamorphosis," Adamov says:

> Le fait que l'homme soit mortel-et redoute la mort, et que
> cette crainte souvent l'obsède-ne l'empêche pas de vivre,
> donc de lutter. Et pas d'histoire: on sait toujours contre
> quoi on lutte, et pourquoi. [6]

Thus his "political" theater in no way denies his vision of man's
ultimate helplessness in an unrecognizable and hostile universe, but
in addition it posits a need to react within this given context against
the curable aspects of the situation. His theater of revolt evolves
toward a theater of revolution. Nor does his political theater abandon

---

[5] Martin Esslin, *The Theatre of the Absurd* (New York, 1961), pp. 72-73.
[6] *Ici et maintenant,* p. 143.

the formal considerations so important to his earlier work. Like
Brecht before him, he recognizes that form is inseparable from substance, that, as Guicharnaud says of the "new" committed playwrights:

> ... it is not enough to offer a traditional presentation of the
> conflicts between worthy proletarians and nasty bosses, but
> that the very structure of the play must also be a revolution-
> ary act. [7]

Not only do we see the carry-over of many avant-garde techniques
and procedures in Adamov's political theater, but more importantly
we witness an ever-present concern for the individual, the particular,
the human element. The dual-dilemma of man's consciousness both of
himself as an individual in an absurd universe and of his role as a
political and historical object in a given situation is preserved with
delicate balance. It is in sustaining this equilibrium that Adamov's
political theater avoids for the most part the dangers of traditional
committed theater, a danger he was acutely aware of and that he
describes in *Ici et Maintenant,* a collection of his essays on theater:

> Je vois un danger... dans un théâtre politique qui, à force
> de refuser les particularités, aboutirait, par un autre chemin,
> au symbolisme qu'il s'efforce de combattre. [8]

Just as in the earlier plays Adamov's characters were the images of
individuals while at the same time they represented man in general,
so in his later theater his characters react differently to the same
situations because they are individuals, specific and complex human
beings, as well as workers, peasants, revolutionaries:

> Deux ouvriers travaillent à la même chaîne, leur condition
> est la même; mais à aliénation égale, leur comportement
> sera différent, selon leur physique-l'un est beau, l'autre est
> laid, l'un grand, l'autre petit — leur vie familiale, leurs
> amours.... [9]

Théâtre de Société, "(scènes d'actualité)," is a collection of five "saynètes politiques," short plays of obvious political orientation: *La
vedette* of Guy Demoy, *La nouvelle constitution* of Maurice Regnaut,

[7] Guicharnaud, p. 206.
[8] *Ici et maintenant,* p. 163.
[9] *Ici et maintenant,* p. 163.

Intimité, Je ne suis pas Français, and *La complainte du ridicule* of Arthur Adamov.

As early as 13 May 1958 Adamov notes in his journal *L'Homme et L'Enfant* the rise of "fascism" in France and Algeria and adds:

> Nous essayons d'écrire des saynètes politiques, dénonçant l'imposture qui vient, mais nous y arrivons mal, le recul manque. [10]

The three short plays represent Adamov's first efforts to deal with what he calls: "a difficult but tempting genre," to find a form wherein man's political role and essential being are balanced cohesively. That each play varies in its approach, tone and techniques bears witness to the continuing evolution of Adamov's theater. But the unifying structural principle of these plays as well as *Les Ames mortes* and *Le Printemps 71* is the representation of man's political and existential struggle within a specific time, place and situation as literally and as grossly as possible. The plays seek to deal then with a current predicament — an obvious departure from the early plays — but in a familiar manner. Adamov explains in the *Avant-Propos*:

> Le "théâtre de société," pour ne pas dire le théâtre politique, est un genre ardu mais tentant. La situation française actuelle (1958), par exemple, avec ses paradoxes apparents, ses retournements grotesques dissimulant l'impeccable logique des intérêts de classe, demande à être *représentée,* et cela le plus littéralement, donc le plus grossièrement possible. [11]

Thus Adamov does not limit himself to a purely "political" theater in the traditional sense of the term, but rather seeks to dramatize man's struggle within an historical and political context, simultaneously aware of man's eternal human condition as well as his specific role or roles in particular social and political situations:

> Beaucoup croient que je veux me borner à un théâtre politique. Ce n'est pas vrai. Ce qui est vrai, c'est la haine que je voue aujourd'hui à des "histoires" coupées de leur contexte social, mutilées, soi-disant "éternelles." [12]

---

[10] Arthur Adamov, *L'Homme et L'Enfant* (Paris, 1968), p. 128.
[11] Arthur Adamov, *Avant-Propos* in *Théâtre de Société* (Paris, 1958),
[12] *Ici et maintenant,* p. 167.

Intimité (1958), the first of the three political sketches, is highly allegorical in style, using personified collective concepts as characters, as well as highly satirical in intent, exposing the manipulations and degradation of power politics. Adamov is rather explicit in the "Avant-Propos in stating his intentions:

> J'ai commencé par écrire *Intimité,* où j'essaie de résumer sous une forme délibérément allégorique la connivence réelle du général de Gaulle avec les factieux et le grand capital. [13]

The short play is divided into two almost equal parts. In the opening section *La Cause incarnée* is the principal guest at an intimate dinner at the home of M. de Ponteville. Others present are M. de Ponteville's friend M. Royal, his nephew L'Élite, and the lackey M. Le Pupille. They are first of all a tightly knit group of people bound together in intimacy by selfish interest. While individually they jockey for more favorable positions within the group, collectively they maintain a strong posture of mutual protection against outside disruptive influences. It is a world wherein people use people to their own advantage, a society in which a person's importance is predicated on his ability to be of use. They are individual stars within a self-contained galaxy, parts of a whole whose sustaining gravitational force is *La Cause incarnée.* His unique importance is quickly established by the opening lines of the play, which are not spoken by the character *La Cause incarnée,* but rather by a record of his voice. *La Cause incarnée* is France, the duty, honor, and destiny of France. The record announces, in what is an obvious and fairly heavy-handed caricature of De Gaulle:

> Français, Françaises, la Cause incarnée, qui n'appartient à personne sinon à la France, a su, au moment le plus terrible de l'Histoire de France, assumer la France. Et, assumant la France, elle est absolument, elle est intégralement, devenue la France. [14]

The respective roles of the others present at the dinner quickly fall in line. M. de Ponteville represents capital, the financial underpinnings of the state, anxious to put the glorious speeches aside so as

---

[13] *Avant-Propos* in *Théâtre de Société,* p. 9.
[14] Arthur Adamov, *Intimité* in *Théâtre de Société* (Paris, 1958), p. 14.

to discuss the important economic situation. M. Royal personifies the elitist spirit of nobility, monarchy, and tradition recognizing the need of the state for the support of the masses, but only as a support, "Oui, les masses dirigées par l'élite, l'élite soutenue par les masses." [15] His nephew, L'Élite, dressed in para-military fashion, represents the storm troopers of totalitarianism, the military solution to the complexities of political and social life. M. le Pupille, the lackey is the subservient socialist republicanism of the Fourth Republic, admitted to the intimate inner circle only because he is needed to serve. He is still learning — and a very willing pupil — from the older more traditional forces of the state, continually compromising himself to curry favor, to stay within the privileged group. He is perhaps the most powerful symbol of the resultant degradation of power politics because in him we see the degradation in process. We see his corruption not as a finished product but as being accomplished. When M. le Pupille is released from the closet by L'Élite because, "On a encore besoin de toi, on te cassera la binette plus tard," he is ecstatic, "C'est le plus beau jour de ma vie!" [16]

Into this lion's den of intrigues and power walks L'Homme qui voit les causes et ressent les effets, a worker in overalls, carrying the sign *Vive la République*. The second part of the play is a dramatic confrontation between the proletariat and the tightly knit group of selfish interests that hides hypocritically behind the banners of nationalism and patriotism. The worker's very presence in the room exposes the machinery of the politics of arrangement which crushes the common man with its greed, its drive for financial, social, and political power. The others are defenseless before the honesty and purity of his laugh. M. de Ponteville feels threatened by his mocking presence and calls on force, Effet de la Cause, to subside the revolutionary laugh. A battle ensues and when L'Homme seems to be gaining the upper-hand and M. le Pupille falters in his support of totalitarian methods, other Effets de la Cause are quickly summoned up to defeat L'Homme. Now La Cause Incarnée can continue uninterrupted the meal in which the privileged castes of the unified front of capital, nobility, and subservient socialism share. For now not only is there a style of government, but even a rhythm of government, a relentless

---

[15] *Intimité*, p. 16.
[16] *Intimité*, p. 20.

pounding of the individual into subservience and degradation. In one of his many "inspired" moments La Cause Incarnée pontificates:

> L'intervention de la destinée humaine dans l'enchaînement des circonstances a quelque chose d'irrévocable. [17]

The hypocritical machinery of "state" has been set in motion. Only the worker is free to revolt against its nefarious corruption and degradation. The original statement of power politics at the dinner party in the opening part of the play is intensified by a series of repetitious demonstrations of that power at work corrupting, degrading at an accelerated pace until it reaches its paroxysm in the necessary destruction of L'Homme.

The familiar structure of intensification reappears in this first of a series of political plays as a natural instrument for unveiling the hidden hypocrisy of a Cause that sacrifices its people for itself. Man is the victim of the play, the object manoeuvered, bought, and sold. And yet man is the only one capable of halting the machinery, of revolting against it by throwing himself into the very machine itself to stop its relentlessly crushing motion. Man, the bartered object of *Le Ping-Pong* and of *Paolo Paoli,* will be the bartered object of *Les Ames mortes* and other plays to come, but now with the added difference that within his given social, political, and historical context he will revolt, he will seek to halt the degrading, destructive machinery of state and system. Thus, while *Intimité* is in itself inferior in many respects to Adamov's other plays, it is important historically in that it marks the playwright's first step in a direction that becomes increasingly more central to his theater.

Je ne suis pas Français, while distinctly "realistic" in style in contrast to the more allegorical *Intimité,* makes fundamentally the same statement as the first play regarding power politics while employing the same basic structure of intensification by repetition. The play depicts Algiers in May of 1958, just after the De Gaulle proclamation of Franco-Mussulman solidarity, and the way in which the French military coerce the Moslems into displaying support of the

---

[17] *Intimité,* p. 17.

government. Adamov describes in the "Avant-Propos" to *Théâtre de Société* the need he felt to dramatize this subject even though he himself had not been in Algeria:

> *Je ne suis pas Français* est peut-être trop schématique, trop'avant-garde'au sens où je n'aime plus ce terme. Mais je voulais absolument parler de cette "fraternisation" franco-musulmane, et, n'ayant pas été en Algérie, j'ai dû me référer aux temoignages de ceux qui en revenaient. Le tableau final m'a été effectivement inspiré par le récit d'un journaliste étranger (libéral). [18]

The short play is divided into three tableaux each of which demonstrates the same persecution and manipulation of the Arabs, but with each tableau growing in intensity by virtue of its parallelism reinforced by moderate variation. The typically bourgeois and chauvinistic Famille-Pied-Noir which insults the Algerian selling peanuts in the opening tableau anticipates the two French paratroopers who coerce the same Algerian to take part in a demonstration for the government of De Gaulle in the second tableau. And interestingly enough this repeated harassment of the manipulated Arab is framed within terms of language. The obstinate silence of the Arab provokes Papa-Pied-Noir:

> Tu sais pas le français, peut-être? Si tu ne sais pas le français, moi, je peux te l'apprendre. [19]

Just as it provokes the two paratroopers:

> Tu ne sais pas le français, peut-être? On peut te l'apprendre, si tu veux? [20]

It is only in the third and final tableau when questioned about franco-mussulman solidarity by the two English journalists that the Arab breaks silence. His only words, repeated with finality and total revolt, are, "Je ne suis pas Français." [21]

---

[18] *Avant-Propos* in *Théâtre de Société*, pp. 9-10.
[19] Arthur Adamov, *Je ne suis pas Français* in *Théâtre de Société* (Paris, 1958), pp. 34-35.
[20] *Je ne suis pas Français*, p. 38.
[21] *Je ne suis pas Français*, p. 44.

But it is more than the silence of the Arab which is the ultimate act of his revolt against and rejection of the totalitarian system being foisted on him. For just as the worker's laugh in *Intimité* had such a disconcerting effect on the powers of state and had to be silenced, so the Arab's look unsettles Papa-Pied-Noir, who wiping his sweaty brow in Tableau I says:

> Moi, je suis Français, et puis je n'aime pas qu'on me regarde comme ce type-là m'a regardé. J'y peux rien, je n'aime pas ça. [22]

He is helpless before "that look" as is the Premier Para of the second tableau who stands paralyzed in front of the Algerian:

> Pourquoi que tu nous regardes comme ça? J'aime pas moi, qu'on nous regarde comme ça! [23]

It is the same look which instills fear even in the relatively neutral English newspaper man:

> A votre place, Harry, je n'interrogerais plus ces musulmans. Vous n'avez peut-être pas remarqué l'étrange regard que cet homme nous a jeté, mais moi, qui suis observateur, je l'ai remarqué. . . . [24]

The crushing machinery of totalitarianism must be halted, the play tells us. The degrading ignominy of a system wherein people are made objects to be manipulated or bartered must be balanced by the simple yet heroic "Je ne suis pas Français" of the persecuted Arab. The laugh of the worker in *Intimité*, the look of the Algerian in *Je ne suis pas Français* is the hope of the future, the rebellion of the present, the necessary stand that man must take if he is ever to live justly. For the imperfect social and political system of which he is the victim is not inherent in the human condition. Thus the fear and paralysis of Papa-Pied-Noir, the Premier Para, and the Premier Journaliste are the first cracks in the mask of ignominious persecution, the beginning of the unmasking of those terrible powers that seem to

---

[22] *Je ne suis pas Français,* pp. 37-38.
[23] *Je ne suis pas Français,* p. 40.
[24] *Je ne suis pas Français,* p. 45.

control man's destiny but in fact are only permitted by man's loss of a sustaining and unifying spiritual dimension.

The power of the Arab to unsettle the paralyzing totalitarianism of the situation rests in the simp'e yet heroic dignity of his refusal to accept the system. His rejection couched in the simple terms, "Je ne suis pas Français," makes him more than just an object of hate and persecution, a victim put-upon by the selfishness of those in power. He becomes a positive point of departure in a universe of uncertainty. And as David Grossvogel points out in his *20th Century French Drama,* this is true of many of Adamov's characters:

> As usual, his human is hardly more than a negative quantity, a victim whose capacity to exist is real only to the extent that the physical instruments of his torture are real and will be used on him: it is only by comparison with these instruments that he is found to have significance greater than that of the rudimentary and static object. [25]

In *La Complainte du Ridicule,* the final playlet of *Théâtre de Société,* it is again language which occupies the central place, which is used, in this case, to contradict and battle against the false language of propaganda and suppression. Adamov describes in the "Avant-Propos" his intention and approach:

> *La Complainte du Ridicule* joue sur les mots. Je me suis demandé si souvent pourquoi le ridicule ne tuait plus que j'ai fini par faire du Ridicule un personnage fatigué. Et puisque la propagande gouvernementale use continuellement d'un langage truqué, pourquoi ne pas lutter contre elle à l'aide du vrai langage? [26]

They play is shaped in the form of a short monologue in which the personification of ridicule, alone on the stage, is being teased and stoned by his supporters off-stage because he is no longer capable of killing. His speech, at first tearful and apologetic, then growing more firm and forceful in tone, is both an explanation of his reduced effectiveness against the political stupidities of the present as well as

---

[25] David I. Grossvogel, *20th Century French Drama* (New York, 1961), p. 323.

[26] *Avant-Propos* in *Théâtre de Société,* p. 9.

a plea for the support of others in his necessary work against pretention and suppression.

The entire speech is divided into three equal parts: (1) a statement of his glorious effectiveness in the past, (2) an explanation for his reduced efficiency in the present, and finally (3) a plea for help against the false republic, war and dire poverty. In the opening section Le Ridicule cites examples from history — Général Boulenger, Colonel de la Rocque, Badinguet and his plebiscite, Maréchal Lebœuf, Monsieur Thiers — as indicative of his energetic youthful pursuit and destruction of enemies of the people by exposure of the falsity, pomposity and ridiculousness of their pretentions:

> Et vous savez aussi combien j'ai travaillé, combien je me suis démené... Vraiment, j'ai la conscience tranquille. Vraiment, j'ai tué tous ceux que j'ai pu... [27]

The central section of the tripartite division concentrates on the present, principally France of 1958, France of the new constitution and Général de Gaulle. Le Ridicule explains the complexity of a situation wherein the ridiculous and the hypocritical are so prevalent amongst both political leaders and their followers that he is at a loss as to where to begin his attack:

> Seulement aujourd'hui, surtout depuis cette nouvelle constitution, j'ai trop à faire, que voulez-vous? Et quand on a trop à faire, quand on est débordé, on est perdu... Frapper, tuer même, au besoin, d'accord! Mais par où commencer, par qui? [28]

Numerous people deserving of his destructive attention are cited, De Gaulle, socialist deputies of a certain type, hypocritical supporters of the referendum, Pineau, Pompidou, Rothschild, Général Chassin. There are so many, just in France alone, that the aging, tiring le Ridicule is incapable of doing the job alone. The ridiculous is so omnipresent that he is even obligated to travel abroad from time to time:

---

[27] Arthur Adamov, *La complainte du ridicule* in *Théâtre de Société* (Paris, 1958), p. 50.

[28] *La complainte du ridicule*, p. 50.

> Sans compter que je suis bien obligé d'aller à l'étranger
> quelquefois, pour entendre Franco parler de la Démocratie,
> ou voir se casser le nez une quelconque petite fusée amé-
> ricaine . . . [29]

In the closing section, he calls upon the aid of his allies in the battle against hypocrisy, totalitarianism and degradation. Le Ridicule cites a recent example of his success, the interruption of De Gaulle's "tournée présidentielle," and credits his minor master-stroke to the support he received from sympathetic forces. For when things become truly serious, when there is shooting or killing, he needs collaboration, friends, and extra effort in order to expose the ridiculous fraud of his enemies to the eyes of the world:

> Quand les choses deviennent sérieuses, quand au truquage
> des paroles s'ajoute, comme en Algérie, la torture des corps,
> comment voulez-vous que tout seul . . .? [30]

The long, entreating harangue, a parody of a typical De Gaulle speech in its phrasing, organization, and emotional appeal, fatigues le Ridicule and he begins to collapse. But the urgency, conviction, and good sense of his words prevail upon the very people who had been casting stones at him at the opening of the play. They come to his rescue, support and maintain him. The fight will go on.

The obvious political content of *La Complainte du Ridicule* as well as the two other "saynètes politiques" of *Théâtre de Société* is rescued from banality and heavy-handedness by a core of humor that punctures the political pretentiousness of those that it attacks. To the degree that this humor is lacking *Je ne suis pas Français* is the least successful of the three plays. In its "realistic" approach, it is the play which takes itself most seriously and forfeits the aesthetic distancing achieved by the humor and caricature of *Intimité* and *La Complainte du Ridicule*. For humor, in the theater of Adamov, is an element, which while perceptible in the early plays, grows in importance in the later plays, reaching its highest point in *M. le Modéré*. It is a humor born of despair, a gesture of defiance against the humiliating ignominy of life, a last defense against life's ultimate

---

[29] *La complainte du ridicule,* p. 50.
[30] *La complainte du ridicule,* pp. 51-52.

degradation, death, or as Adamov himself describes, an antidote against suicide: "Cerné par le malheur, il fallait que j'éclate de rire ou me suicide." [31]

The political playlets of *Théâtre de Société,* while circumscribed in scope, schematic in structure, and limited in objective, point the way in the theater of Adamov towards the more ambitious, complex, fleshed-out political dramas of *Les Ames mortes* and *Le Printemps 71.*

Les Ames mortes, 1960, is an adaptation for the stage of Gogol's famous novel *Dead Souls.* It is both interesting and informative that Adamov chose to adapt a novel for his first full-length political play. Being the capable critic that he was, Adamov was fully aware of the perils of adaptation:

> Les dimensions de la prose ne sont pas celles du théâtre, et vouloir rendre littéralement, dans l'espace physique, les actes qui se déroulent dans un autre espace me semble presque toujours aberrant. [32]

But Adamov, always the playwright, constantly in search of how best to utilize the physical space of the stage and always acutely conscious of the genre in which he worked and by which he sought to represent "literally" his vision of man in the world, recognized, like Gogol himself, the poetic dimensions of *Dead Souls*:

> ...les Ames mortes ne sont pas un roman, mais, comme Gogol l'indiquait lui-même, un poème. Je traduis en langage du XXe siècle, et je dis: une épopée. C'est en effet parce que les aventures de Tchitchikov débordent, et de loin, le cadre romanesque, que je me suis permis de les en faire sortir. [33]

But perhaps most importantly it was the dual-orientation of Gogol's work, its fusion of sharp social and political criticism with intense, personal poetry that captivated Adamov and led him to find in *Dead Souls* a synthesis parallel to that toward which his own work was striving:

---

[31] Arthur Adamov, *Note préliminaire* in *Théâtre IV* (Paris, 1968), p. 11.
[32] Arthur Adamov, *Introduction* in *Les ames mortes* (Paris, 1960), p. 7.
[33] *Introduction* in *Les ames mortes,* p. 7.

> De plus, *Les Ames mortes* se situant constamment au point
> d'intersection d'une critique sociale aiguë et de la poésie qui,
> dans la multiplicité des faits, choisit le fait révélateur, il
> m'est apparu qu'elles ne sont pas étrangères au théâtre dont
> nous avons actuellement le plus besoin: un théâtre épique
> et critique. [34]

Les Ames mortes, while an adaptation, achieves its own originality
of form and statement; unlike Adamov's translations, *La Mort de
Danton* of Büchner in 1948 and *Les Petits Bourgeois* of Gorki in
1959, it deserves inclusion as an authentic and personal dramatic
statement in any systematic study of Adamovian dramaturgy.

The long play which centers around the adventures of Tchitchikov
in Czarist Russia of the nineteenth century is divided into two parts
of approximately the same length with seven and eight tableaux re-
spectively. The "Première Partie," which describes the arrival of
Tchitchikov in a small Russian town, his social and economic con-
quests, and his strange pursuit of "dead souls" might be sub-titled
"The Rise of Tchitchikov." He is the polished, sophisticated outsid-
er, the city man come to the provinces, the new center of attraction
and emulation. The limited social universe of the play revolves around
him: women want to dance with him, the important men of the
society, the Gouverneur, wealthy landowners, the Président du Tribunal, the Directeur des Postes want to talk to him. But underneath
the attractive veneer of civilization Tchitchikov is a man possessed,
a man whose energies are controlled by a singular obsession, that of
buying up the "dead souls" of the region. Adamov explains the play
on words of the title on which the play is built:

> La pièce (comme le roman) repose sur un terrible "jeu de
> mots." Dans la Russie tsariste, on appelait "ames mortes"
> les serfs de sexe masculin sur lesquels les propriétaires fon-
> ciers payaient un impôt. [35]

This tax had to be paid for each serf on the census rolls, whether
he was living or not. Thus the political system of the time had created
a situation whereby, for whatever his own personal reasons, Tchitchi-

---

[34] *Introduction* in *Les ames mortes,* pp. 7-8.
[35] *Ici et maintenant,* p. 115.

kov found most landowners eager to sell at a low price the dead
"dead souls" for which they were accountable.

Five of the opening seven tableaux are variations of the same
basic quest, Tchitchikov's buying of dead souls, his exploitation of a
currupt system for his own benefit. But throughout the entire "Première Partie" we, like the landowners of the play, are never permitted
to fathom his true motive, to understand why it would be advantageous
for him to "own" dead serfs for whom he would be forced to pay
a tax. What we see, however, are the avaricious landowners eager to
benefit from Tchitchikov's strange obsession, bargaining as though the
commodity where real, dealing in people as though they were products.
Korobatchka hesitates to sell, fearing that perhaps the market for
dead souls will rise. Nozdriov prefers to gamble over them and even
cheats at play. Sobakievitch hints at the illegality of the sale so as to
raise the price. And as they try, each in his own way to use Tchitchikov and his obsession to their advantage, so Tchitchikov slowly,
coldly, and with intense calculation manipulates the landowners to
serve his own needs. Moreover, there is always lurking in the background the ultimate morbid irony of their dealings, the fact that the
product of exchange is dead souls.

As Tchitchikov's fortunes rise with increasing regularity from
tableau to tableau in the "Première Partie," so they begin to fall and
disintegrate in the "Deuxième Partie." Once his scheme has been
exposed as formally illegal, there is a direct parallelism-in-reverse
between his descent towards disgrace and his earlier rise to fame
and fortune. Just as each tableau of the "Première Partie" repeatedly
portrayed an increasingly successful deal for dead souls, so each
tableau of the "Deuxième Partie" exposes a Tchitchikov more and
more humiliated, the object of more and more pernicious rumors.

And as the first ball at the Gouverneur's house in the "Première
Partie" marked the beginning of Tchitchikov's ascent to power and
wealth, so it is the second ball at the Gouverneur's house in the
"Deuxième Partie" that signals the beginning of his fall from grace.
For it is at this social gathering, Tchitchikov's moment of triumph,
that the drunken Nozdriov exposes Tchitchikov's clever game in
front of the Gouverneurs and other notables. Each succeeding scene
announces a new rumor, increasingly greater in scope and more
pernicious in nature, to explain the mystery of his buying of dead
souls. The women Anna Grigorievna and Sofia Ivanova interpret his

dealings as a subterfuge whereby to make off with the Gouverneur's daughter. The town officials fear that Tchitchikov is really an inspector sent by the Gouverneur General and traveling incognito to check the irregularities of their district. The Directeur des Postes and Bégouchkine see in Tchitchikov the unidentified counterfeiter known to be at large in their district. Each interprets Tchitchikov and his plan differently and in keeping with his own fears and frustrations. But they are all agreed that the buying of dead souls was only a strategy.

Rumor leads to rumor as rumor contradicts rumor and leads to general confusion:

Le Maître de Police

Arrêter Tchitchikov, comme suspect.

L'Inspecteur des Services d'Hygiène

Et si c'était tout de même l'envoyé du Gouverneur Général?

Le Maître de Police

Ce qui, après tout, n'est pas absolument impossible. Exact.

Le Procureur

Mais si Tchitchikov n'est... ni l'envoyé du Gouverneur... ni un vrai conseiller de collège... ni un vrai faux-monnayeur... ni... ni un bandit, alors que peut-il bien...? [36]

The rumors and resultant confusion continue to mount from tableau to tableau. Some declare that Tchitchikov is really le capitaine Kopékine, a hero of the campaign of 1812, who unlike Tchitchikov, however, had only one leg and one arm. Others think it is more likely that he is really Napoleon set loose in Russia by the English. They take their confusion to Nozdriov who explains that Tchitchikov is (1) a spy, (2) a counterfeiter, (3) a man who intended to seduce the Gouverneur's daughter and (4) that their suspicions that he is Napoleon might just be the right explanation for Tchitchikov's frequent absences as a boy from school.

---

[36] Arthur Adamov, *Les ames mortes* (Paris, 1960), p. 185.

Confusion creates fear and the Procureur dies of fright. When Tchitchikov realizes the seriousness of his predicament, he prepares to flee, but is then put under arrest to appear before the Gouverneur Général. Once in prison Tchitchikov begs the Protopope for aid, revealing at the same time his true motive for dealing in dead souls:

> Bien sûr, se faire prêter de l'argent, beaucoup d'argent par le Conseil de tutelle sur des âmes... inexistantes... n'est ni... licite... ni moral. [37]

But he also makes clear that his plot was spawned by a corrupt system that failed to take into account a man's life, that looked upon serfs as numbers to be taxed whether living or dead:

> Oui, est-ce de ma faute si un jour, quand j'étais fondé de pouvoir, et que, employé consciencieux, je m'inquiétais de savoir quels serfs étaient vivants et quels autres morts, le secrétaire m'a dit: (Prenant une voix froide, administrative.) "D'accord, les uns naissent, les autres meurent, mais pourquoi vous inquiéter, Pavel Ivanovitch? Puisqu'ils figurent tous sur la liste de recensement, et que le compte se retrouve toujours. Le secrétaire était estimé par ses supérieurs, je voulais l'être aussi. Oui, tout... tout le mal vient de ce secrétaire. [38]

A promise of repentence and the offer of financial reimbursement convince the Protopope of Tchitchikov's sincerity and elicit from him a guarantee of help. But it is finally the Maître de Police, in league with the other town notables, who frees Tchitchikov, returns him his money-box, tears up the evidence of the confiscated acts of sale, and advises him to flee as quickly and as far off as possible. He does all this in the name of order, harmony, friendship and thirty thousand roubles.

Thus the rise and fall of Tchitchikov is complete. His short-lived passage through the provincial Russian town has changed nothing. The system has simply absorbed another experience, another victim. The final scene of the play testifies to Adamov's dramatic acuity, for not only does it bring the adventures of Tchitchikov full

---

[37] *Les ames mortes*, p. 216.
[38] *Les ames mortes*, p. 217.

circle within the confines of the play, but it anticipates the encompas-
sing circular pattern of Tchitchikov's subsequent life from province to
province. Adamov explains his choice of ending in *Ici et Maintenant*:

> Chacun sait que *Les Ames mortes* n'ont pas de fin. Or, au
> théâtre, il faut bien finir, et je n'ai pas trouvé de fin qui me
> paraisse à la fois plus scénique et plus *juste* que l'arrestation
> dérisoire de Tchitchikov, rapidement suivie d'une libération
> obtenue à prix d'or. Cette fin ne laisse-t-elle pas supposer,
> d'ailleurs, le prochain recommencement du voyage, des trac-
> tations, des victoires, des dangers, et une autre arrestation,
> dans une autre petite ville de l'immense Russie? [39]

The repetitive structure of intensification which is the informing
principle of Adamov's theater is ideally suited to translate from one
medium to another the poetry of Gogol's novel. The rising crescendo
of the "Première Partie," the systematic buying of dead souls, financial security and social prestige intensifies by its repetition with
variation the sameness of the quest with its concomitant absence of
human values in the bargaining for souls. Adamov explains how the
structure of the play reinforces its thematic statement:

> Même si l'on me reproche une progression trop linéaire, je
> crois qu'il était nécessaire de faire défiler systématiquement
> ces propriétairs apparement différents les uns des autres,
> mais semblables du seul fait de leur souci commun: s'enri-
> chir au maximum, exploiter *tout ce qui peut être exploitable*. [40]

This series of deals for dead souls in the "Première Partie," this
initial pattern of repetition whose intensity is heightened by virtue of
the varying but increasingly successful results, is further intensified
by the parallelism of the decrescendo of the "Deuxième Partie." Here
the scenes become in effect repetitions or semi-repetitions of each
other, variations of the initial accusation against Tchitchikov growing
in seriousness and to such ridiculous proportions as to become ludicrous. Yet it is this pattern of accusation which causes his ultimate
downfall, disgrace, imprisonment and reprieve. A victim of the
system, Tchitchikov supports the system so as to be free to victimize

---

[39] *Ici et maintenant*, p. 114.
[40] *Ici et maintenant*, p. 113.

others. Thus the circular patterns within the play are further reinforced by our awareness that they are but the first in a hypothetical
series of circular patterns throughout the apparently infinite spaces
of Czarist Russia.

The play, by using the "epic" structure of Tchitchikov's odyssey
in search of dead souls, accuses a system so corrupt, so inhuman as
to permit such a person as Tchitchikov, a character who in turn
exposes the system by pushing to its ultimate absurdity or illogicality
the apparently acceptable established political order of Czarist Russia.
It is a political system of servitude, of bondage of man by man, a
system wherein the principal product of exchange is implicitly and
explicitly man, wherein peasants whether dead or alive are referred
to as "dead souls," a system wherein there could be no authentic
life. In a sense Tchitchikov is the most sympathetic of the manip-
ulators in this political and social order because he is the least successful. In trying to be part of the ruling elite, he fails, but in so
doing, he pushes to the extreme the consequences of this inherently
vicious system and thus becomes its greatest critic.

The play is then a political play, for not only does it condemn
man's use of man for his own ends as do *Le Ping-Pong* and *Paolo
Paoli,* where man was only implicitly the real product of exchange,
but it indicts a system, an established order where man as product
of exchange was both politically and morally acceptable. The play
succeeds in denouncing this "legitimate" system by showing its ultimate consequences and inherent absurdity, by demonstrating literally and in concrete images the ultimate viciousness of a system which
man in his inhumanity had grown accustomed to accepting as natural
and logical.

In the final analysis the "dead souls" of the play are then not only
the serfs bought and sold, but the dead in spirit who deal in these
dead souls. The illegitimate quest of Tchitchikov to buy dead "dead
souls" is the ultimate irony of a system whose corruption is so complete that the purchase of living "dead souls" is legitimate. To
preserve itself, the political system gives the appearances of absorbing
and invalidating the adventures of Tchitchikov, while in reality it
frees him to victimize others. Therein lies the ultimate victory of
the existing political order. For rather than collapse before the onslaught of Tchitchikov's *reduction ad absurdum,* it temporarily anes-

thetizes its victim-accuser by permitting him to play a minor role in the system, albeit somewhere else, and thereby permitting the political order to propagate itself. To the extent that *Les Ames mortes* describes an historically accurate form of exploitation and dehumanization in Czarist Russia of the nineteenth century, the play is historical. But its appeal reaches beyond the purely descriptive level. While grounded in history, *Les Ames mortes* with its symbolic overtones speaks to our own age wherein men and systems still exploit and dehumanize other men.

The seriousness of the play's statement on man's inhuman use of man and the trenchant criticism of a political system wherein man is the chief product for sale is at one and the same time thematically intensified but tonally alleviated by the humor and poetry of many of the play's images. The use of film projections of Tchitchikov traveling across the immense open spaces of Russia and its desolate countryside spotted occasionally with isolated villages adds a dimension of timelessness and continuity to his odyssey. They reinforce poetically the empty but relentless quest of man for domination over man. The opening and closing images of the play, Tchitchikov's troika against a void of immense, desolate space, encircle spatially and temporally his adventures within the immense, desolate spaces of human degradation and absence of authentic human values of the play's universe just as the images of desolate countryside between tableaux in the "Première Partie" encircle his separate adventures into individual, desolate domains.

The play on words on which the play is built is sustained and deepened by the growing humor of Adamov which, though "black," rescues the play from a deadening gravity inimical to the play's dual thrust. It makes of *Les Ames mortes* a political play which avoids the pitfalls of its genre. Humor raises *Les Ames mortes* above the simple but heavy-handed formula of "class against class" melodrama by preserving the humanity and complexity of its characters. It makes them more than one-dimensional political beings. The humor springs for the most part from the familiar Adamovian device of using exalted language to describe banal proceedings, or the exact reverse, ordinary, banal terminology to describe extraordinary situations. The crafty, bargaining Korobotchka, anxious to reap even greater profits, hesitates to sell her dead souls and uses a typical formula of sale's resistance,

"D'autres marchands viendront." [41] It is only when we realize what is the subject of sale that the incongruity of the words demands our critical but amused appraisal. Familiar expressions are sometimes inverted to achieve unfamiliar and humorous effect. In a fit of impatience to close a deal, Tchitchikov reworks to his own advantage a traditional Christian expression, "Laissez donc en paix les vivants, Dieu les bénisse! Je vous parle des morts." [42] Not only is the inversion humorous, but it transmits the inverted values of the play's universe. It sums up and exposes by caricature and poetic distance the absurdity of the norms people live by. Humor in language in *Les Ames mortes* is the key to this mechanism of critical exposure while at the same time it keeps the play from being a fruitless and heavy-handed exercise in political satire.

Le Printemps 71 marks the final stage of Adamov's development within the political plays of the years 1958-1961. Of all his major plays it is the most overtly political in nature while at the same time it represents his most advanced and complex attempt to synthesize techniques from the two major orientations within his work, the avant-garde theater of derision and the Brechtian epic-realist theater.

The play is based on the history of the short-lived Paris Commune of 1871, when the working classes seized control of Paris, the Bank of France, and means of production on the 18th of March. It describes the rise and fall of the Commune with its eventual destruction on the 28th of May of the same year by the regular French army of the government of Thiers with the assistance of Bismarck, his Prussian troops, as well as sympathetic French reactionaries working inside the city. Within this broad historical framework, Adamov creates a play which, while basically simple in structure, is extremely rich in texture. It portrays some thirty-six possible political positions, ranging from cautious liberalism to the militant marxism of the late nineteenth century, as well as numerous personal dramas intertwined within the major political drama.

The play, Adamov's longest, is divided into three acts which in turn are divided into 26 tableaux. Act I represents the Commune triumphant, her enemies provisionally in flight to Versailles. Act II

---

[41] *Les ames mortes,* p. 68.
[42] *Les ames mortes,* p. 66.

is the Commune in its first stages of disintegration, slowly losing control of the city and its people by a series of political errors and betrayals. Act III shows the dissolution and destruction of the Commune, its ultimate victimization by the system. This broad historical outline is, however, only the canvas on which Adamov paints the essential dramas of man's struggle within history and against the systems he has created. It is the "petite manœuvre" enlarged but still symbolic rather than essential to his statement of man's oppression of man. For though historical, the play does not concentrate on the grand designs of its period, spotlighting the famous and infamous leaders known to the conventional history texts. It is rather a play about the political evolution of the little people who made up the Commune, their understanding of its political significance, and the drama of their relationship to the Commune's efforts to throw off the shackles of subjugation and political ignominy.

This dual orientation of the play is advanced and formally defined by a repetitive structure of intensification created by the juxtaposition of the numerous "realistic" tableaux depicting personal or individual dramas of relationship and political evolution and the nine "allegorical" interludes or "guignols" which outline the political and historical thrust of the play. It is only in the "guignols," for example, that the principal historical characters of the Commune and its suppression appear — Thiers, Bismarck, etc. — while at the same time the societal and political forces of the period such as the Bank of France, the National Assembly and even the Commune itself appear as allegorical characters. The "guignols" are frequently humorous but principally they depict the grand historical lines of the three-month Commune, thereby freeing the tableaux for the play's dominant concern, the study of the people, their personal dilemmas, their relationships to each other, and of course, their evolving relationship to the Commune and its principles. It is they who elicit, as Geneviève Serreau points out in her *Histoire du nouveau théâtre,* our interest, sympathy and pity:

> Adamov mit sur scène dans *Le Printemps 71* le petit peuple de la Commune, les ouvriers de Paris "tels qu'ils étaient, gais, travailleurs, turbulents, héroïques," requérant du spectateur et son adhésion et sa sympathie et sa pitié. En contrepoint, les "guignols" versaillais, inspirés par les dessins de Daumier, apparaissent en des "intermèdes allégoriques"

> chargés surtout de faire le point des événements qui préci-
> pitèrent le sanglant affrontement. [43]

The people, the citizens of Paris, are not only those like Robert, Jeanne-Marie, and Pierre who are willing to give their life so that the idea of freedom might live, but they are also those like Anatole who worry only about the possible destruction of their personal possessions. They are people who fall in love and people who become jealous and hate. There are those who make political decisions based on political considerations and those who act politically for personal or sentimental reasons. Pierre explains to Robert the truth of his decision to go to defend the Préfecture:

> Tu vas à la Préfecture parce que Polia y va, et Polia parce
> qu'elle s'inquiète pour Sofia. [44]

There are those like Sofia and Polia for whom the ultimate importance is the continued struggle of the working classes for liberation, and those like the bourgeois Pécheteau for whom the major concern is:

> ... que les ateliers Pécheteau passent des mains de Péche-
> teau père aux mains de Pécheteau fils. [45]

They are a people confused and giddy with the expectation of success, citizens who are incapable of recognizing the truth of their political and military situation. A soldier of the Commune, wounded in the battle at Clamart, is at the center of the deception when he says:

> Je n'ai pas peur ... Mais je pense à Clamart, tout le temps.
> Si tu savais! ... quelle déroute ... Et à Paris, on parlait de
> nos victoires. [46]

When the collapse of the city is imminent, there is not only despair and faultfinding, courage and fear, but vanity and frivolity. The baroness Sibylle excitedly searches for Monsieur Beaubourg of the newspaper Le Figaro:

---

[43] Geneviève Serreau, Histoire du "nouveau théâtre" (Paris, 1966), p. 79.
[44] Arthur Adamov, Le Printemps 71 (Paris, 1961), p. 113.
[45] Le Printemps 71, p. 154.
[46] Le Printemps 71, p. 162.

> Il m'a promis que j'aurais ma binette dans *Le Figaro*: la
> première petite baronne dans Paris encore insurgé. [47]

The man who once sold newspapers sympathetic to the Commune
now sells reactionary papers that herald the triumph of Thiers and
the forces of Versailles. He excuses his defection of grounds of prac-
tical necessity:

> J'ai deux petits à la maison, et ils ont faim. [48]

The Commune, the people of the Commune, turns inward in a
moment of agonizing reappraisal and soul-searching to discover its
mistakes. It is a time of second-guessing, fault-finding, and eventually
self-recrimination. It is Jeanne-Marie, always zealous but frequently
critical who now best sums up the situation:

> On a tous fait des fautes. Moi, la première. Si on avait osé
> occuper la Banque, ils n'auraient jamais, jamais . . . osé occu-
> per Paris. C'est Sofia qui avait raison. [49]

All these individual dramas of relationship and evolution which
take place within and become part of the great historical conflict of
the future against the past, of the Republic against the Monarchy are
victimized not only by the tyranny of the political system that crushes
them, but also by the tyranny of time, a time much too brief for the
numerous tasks confided to the Commune and its partisans. The drama
of this exemplary moment in the history of man's struggle upward
is intensified and humanized by its temporal dimension, its built-in
"theatrical" time of only 73 days, by the contraction of so much political, historical and human drama into such a short period of time.
Adamov underlines the importance of the temporal dimension as he
explains in *Ici et maintenant* his attraction to the Commune:

> La Commune me paraît un événement particulièrement im-
> portant, tant du point de vue politique que du point de vue
> strictement dramatique. Tant de grands pressentiments,
> d'erreurs, de combats *sur tous les fronts,* et en si peu de

---

[47] *Le Printemps 71,* p. 219.
[48] *Le Printemps 71,* p. 223.
[49] *Le Printemps 71,* p. 211.

temps ... C'est peut-être cette question du temps, du manque de temps, ce resserrement terrible des choses, en soixante-treize jours, qui m'a le plus intéressé, le plus frappé. [50]

Thus we see that Adamov regarded the Commune of 1871 as important from a political point of view as well as dramatically captivating. The "poésie folle" of the Commune, its heroism, its abortive and naive attempt to cure political and social evils, *le mal curable*, was inspirational but also instructive. For the first time in history, Adamov observed, men defended their own fate, power was held by the working classes over the means of production:

> Le premier gouvernment ouvrier, le courage, l'intelligence, puis l'héroïsme qui ont fait de Paris durant trois mois la capitale du monde, n'y a-t-il pas là l'un des plus grands sujects de théâtre? [51]

But the play is not only an heroic hymn to the Commune and the "little people" of Paris. It is also a realistic play which criticizes their errors as well, errors which we see depicted in the squabblings, indecisions and petty jealousies within the tableaux:

> En d'autres termes, j'ai tenu donc à ce que *Le Printemps 71* soit une pièce critique, et qui tienne compte de tout ce que nous avons appris depuis, et en grande partie grâce à la Commune. [52]

Yet even in this most advanced of "political" plays in which the *mal curable* is most obviously the central concern, the play continues to mingle Adamov's two dominant preoccupations of inner and exterior conflict, of the psychological as well as the political dimension, and of the individual as well as the class struggle. And once again it is this concern for the lost unifying spiritual dimension of man — along with certain technical procedures — which saves the play from that particular sort of simplistic symbolism so common to historico-political drama and which Adamov so consciously sought to avoid:

---

[50] *Ici et maintenant,* p. 118.
[51] *Ici et maintenant,* p. 145.
[52] *Ici et maintenant,* p. 122.

> ... j'ai essayé de bannir le symbolisme et de raconter une
> très simple histoire qui tienne compte à la fois des éléments
> psychologiques et aussi des éléments politiques. Ce qui m'a
> attiré dans la Commune, c'est le rapport qui existait alors
> entre la vie privée et la vie politique. [53]

The drama of the Commune is the drama of the people, of the individual men and women who collectively created the political evolution
of France in 1871. The emphasis within the play is therefore not on
the celebrated heroes and villains of history, but on the particular
evolution of each and every man within the general political situation.

In a very real sense the drama of the Commune is the drama of
Robert Marpeaux multiplied, for *Le Printemps 71* is that "political"
play of Adamov which promotes most the direction outlined by the
transitional work *Paolo Paoli*. The solitary, evolutionary character of
Marpeaux is here more extensively defined and developed as the
working class in revolt against its suppression. The commodities of
Paolo Paoli, both real and apparent, are more specifically political in
Le Printemps 71 as are the terms of the conflict. The individual Communards are made more believeable and sympathetic. Yet *Le Printemps 71* fulfills to a great degree the promise contained in *Paolo
Paoli.* It combines on both a thematic and formal level and with a
certain degree of success elements of the Theater of the Absurd as
well as components of the epic-realist theater of criticism.

Moreover, man is still the victim and therefore, ultimately, the
oppressor. The system which dehumanizes him is man-made — *le mal
curable* — and is an extension of the inner conflict proceeding from
man's loss of the spiritual or unifying dimension. The thematic evolution of Adamov's theater within the "political plays" lies in man's
refusal to accept the blind victimization and dehumanization that he
once endured as inescapable. He now mobilizes his forces against
those aspects of life which can be challenged. For from the earliest
plays to the very last the theater of Adamov never varies from its
core, man's victimization and ignominy. It is only the attitude toward
his condition which evolves and becomes the redeeming factor, as
Guicharnaud notes in his *Modern French Theater*:

---

[53] *Ici et maintenant*, p. 129.

If the individual is a victim, it is because the social system can be maintained only by anti-Kantian procedure. Adamov's plays are all centered on that blind victimization (*La grande et la petite manœuvre,* for example) or on a refusal of it (*Le Printemps 71*) as well as on an aesthetic revenge: The playwright himself transforms into objects — that is, into puppets — the social forces that feed on the dehumanization of man. [54]

---

[54] Guicharnaud, p. 202.

Chapter V

THE SOCIAL PLAYS

The common denominator of Adamov's last five plays *La Politique des Restes* (1962), *Sainte Europe* (1966), *M. le Modéré* (1967), *Off Limits* (1968), and *Si l'été revenait* (1970), is that their dimensions are essentially social. All five plays are principally concerned with the social systems of alienated modern society, their viciousness, perversions, degradation and inauthenticity.

La Politique des Restes denounces the social system of apartheid as practiced in South Africa. *Sainte Europe* is a caricature of our Western life-style, its triviality, commercialism and lack of authentic positive heroes. *M. le Modéré* exposes by mockery a social system devoid of grace and poetry wherein the imagination is condemned as antithetical to the needs of reasonable men in reasonable society. *Off Limits* speaks of the anguish of the "American" way of life, of an America sick of America, of America as the fullest expression of contemporary society's malaise before the void and ignominy of the modern age. It is an age without faith, the age Adamov defines already in *L'Aveu* as a time of ignominy, an epoch summed up in the single word "degradation," a time in which man has lost the unifying spiritual dimension of the old, forgotten myths:

> Sagesse insondable des mythes et des rites du vieux monde mort! Toute la folie environnante n'est rien d'autre que le vertige engendré par le vide que laisse au cœur de l'homme l'oubli des cultes millénaires. [1]

---

[1] Arthur Adamov, *L'Aveu* (Paris, 1946), p. 111.

The five plays are penetrated with the prevailing despair of the times. Their latent thematic identity proceeds from modern man's failure to create a new unifying myth to fill the void in a world of absence, absence of *a priori* values, absence of communication, absence of personal dignity, and in these plays most especially, the absence of man's awareness of and concern for his fellow man as they live together in society. Some twenty years earlier Adamov, writing in *L'Aveu,* had already recognized the emptiness of modern life which he depicts in these five plays:

> Je ne suis pas voué à la tâche gigantesque de la création du mythe à venir. Mais je dois dire très haut ce que je sais. Crier que le mal qui ronge le monde et s'agrandit sans cesse prend racine au lieu même-lieu au cœur de tout mal-où gît le cadavre géant des mythes des origines. [2]

Another unifying factor in this final phase of Adamov's theater is the thrust of these five plays towards a more authentic reconciliation of the divergent forms of his work. Having developed to their fullest in *Le Printemps 71* the epic-realist possibilities announced in *Paolo Paoli,* Adamov's ensuing theater re-examines and re-incorporates certain formal considerations of his earlier work. As Geneviève Serreau points out in her *Histoire du "nouveau theatre,"* it is for Adamov a moment of self-questioning and renewal:

> Après *Le Printemps 71...* Adamov fut amené à s'interroger de plus en plus précisément sur le sens de ses propres démarches et à se situer, dans sa particularité, par rapport au théâtre politique où il venait de s'engager et par rapport à ce "théâtre de l'absurde" dont il avait été naguère l'un des plus solides défenseurs. [3]

For in abandoning the purely ethical protest of his earlier work in favor of a developing political conscience in the transitional plays, Adamov's theater falls victim in the political plays to a certain timidity of form and conformity in language, an excess of "realism" inimical to his talent. It is a type of strait-jacket self-imposed, a protection against the anarchistic energies of his absurdist view that might im-

---

[2] *L'Aveu,* p. 154.
[3] Geneviève Serreau, *Histoire du "nouveau théâtre"* (Paris, 1966), pp. 80-81.

pinge upon and obscure the ideology he espouses and wishes to express. It is a fear, Roland Barthes explains in his *Essais critiques,* common to those whose theater maintains a political commitment:

> L'un des grands dangers du théâtre politique, c'est la peur de tomber dans le formalisme bourgeois: cette hantise aveugle au point de renvoyer dans l'excès contraire: le théâtre réaliste succombe trop souvent sous la timidité de la dramaturgie, le conformisme du langage; par suspicion de l'anarchie, on en vient facilement à endosser les vieilles formes usées du théâtre bourgeois, sans comprendre que c'est la matérialité même du théâtre, et non seulement l'idéologie, qui doit être repensée. [4]

In his final five plays Adamov succeeds in reconciling not only the formal divergencies of "avant-garde" and epic-realist dramaturgy, but the thematic duality of "absurdist" and "political" orientation. He moves, as in his masterpiece, *Le Ping Pong,* towards a synthesis of form and content, a union of style and view that is particularly his own, like no other, and that takes into account both man in the universe and man in society. Adamov expresses his aim as follows:

> J'ai voulu, avec *La Politique des Restes* et *Sainte Europe* ... retrouver mon ancien théâtre dit "d'avant-garde" et que j'ai, il est vrai, beaucoup décrié. Mais je crois que, dans ces dernières pièces — et quelles que soient les ressemblances évoquées —, j'ai uni, réuni, un peu mieux que dans le passé, la psychologie de chacun et la ligne générale, *politique,* de tous. [5]

La Politique des Restes is ideally suited to transmit this dual concern of Adamov for the psychology of the individual and the "ligne generale, politique, de tous." Within the framework of a conventional murder trial with traditional flashbacks, the play establishes a parallel or analogy between the protagonist's personal psychosis — the fear of detritus — and the collective psychosis of the society in which he lives, racism.

Johnny Brown, a white factory owner in South Africa, stands trial for the murder of Tom Guinness, a black worker at the factory. We learn by a series of intermittent flashbacks that the protagonist had

---

[4] Roland Barthes, *Essais critiques* (Paris, 1964), p. 82.
[5] Arthur Adamov, *Introduction* in *Théâtre III* (Paris, 1966), p. 9.

suffered a mental collapse resulting from his pathological fear of the multiplicity of things — too many things in the world, too many seasons, days, hours, trains, tickets, but especially too much trash and garbage, the remains of cigarettes, pealings, cut finger-nails — and he arrives at the conclusion that all of this refuse is being accumulated for him to swallow. His particular psychosis, his personal fear of the mounting piles of refuse, parallels the collective fear of the privileged white class of South African apartheid society to which he belongs, a class which fears the growing number and eventual liberation and take-over by the Blacks. A victim of his milieu as well as his own obsession, Johnny confuses and confounds his fear of persecution by waste with that of persecution by Blacks, arriving at the insanely logical conclusion that he can put an end to the one persecution by ending the other. He kills a Black.

Yet the drama of his trial for the murder of Tom Guinness, while it relates and dramatizes by flashback the sickness of the protagonist and resultant murder of an innocent man, is also the drama of collusion and inequity; the trial of a society devoted to the preservation of the notion that man, in this case the Blacks, is an object to be used and destroyed at will. The trial epitomizes a social system of degradation wherein the sickest person, the murderer, enjoys impunity, does not have to suffer the results of his action, because his class controls that society with its means of production and its means of justice.

The man on trial is only apparently accused, for the entire proceedings are an exercise in acquittal, a mockery structured to preserve the appearances of justice and the superiority of the white race. The complicity of judge, prosecutor, defense attorney and witnesses is the final triumph of a closed society determined to protect its own, no matter how criminal or aberrant their behavior. When the Defense in summation, having cited Johnny's past as a rich, honorable and respectable man as well as his contribution to the State and its citizens by virtue of his factory's production of sulfuric acid, concludes that he must not now suffer prison life, the presiding judge is surprised and distressed at the very mention of prison, and hastily counters, "Mais qui . . . a parlé de prison?" [6] For there has never been

---

[6] Arthur Adamov, *La Politique des Restes* in *Théâtre III* (Paris, 1966), p. 179.

a shadow of doubt concerning the ultimate "innocence" of the accused. Although he has openly admitted shooting Tom, he cannot be judged guilty of murder since the victim was a Black, a thing, an object. It remains for the court only to determine the degree of guilt involved and the concomitant punishment. The Prosecutor, who for the most part, directs the trial even to the point of manipulating the Judge and the Defense Attorney, accuses Johnny of a crime of passion, an excess of fervor, reacting more vigorously than others to the proliferation of Blacks, and demands a punishment of seven months imprisonment with reprieve. Johnny's Defense Attorney describes this as excessive and seeks an acquittal pure and simple.

But Johnny is not just a white racist in an apartheid society, a symbol in a simplistic class struggle. He is more than just one more product of a system whose social fabric corrupts, degrades and destroys. He is also a madman with a wife and brother who hope to profit both financially and amourously from his madness by sending him back to a sanitarium and taking over control of the factory. James and Joan Brown, we learn in a flashback, had tried to bribe Dr. Perkins to keep Johnny in his mental clinic. Perkins had refused their money, diagnosing Johnny's illness as merely an exaggerated form of the fear prevalent in the white community:

> Enfin, que cette sensation de reste... n'était, somme toute, que l'exagération d'une sensation assez généralement ressentie par beaucoup de blancs dans notre état. Et cela est compréhensible, se sentant d'une race et d'une catégorie sociale sur lesquelles pourraient un jour peser certaines menaces...[7]

But James and Joan do succeed in bribing a witness, Mr. Galao, Johnny's former barber and a white man, who testifies that Johnny attacked him after his release from the clinic. While not always cognizant of certain specific details, Johnny is acutely aware of their conspiracy against him, and describes them to the court as being financially and amorously united:

> ...accusez alors ma très chère épouse, pour la très simple et bonne raison qu'afin de coucher avec mon très cher frère, et surtout, je dis bien surtout, de m'évincer de la direction

---

[7] *La Politique des Restes,* p. 155.

de mes affaires, elle complota, je veux dire, ils complotèrent,
pour que lesdites affaires, noyées dans je ne sais quelle grosse
affaire, véreuse, honteuse . . . [8]

It is James and Joan, however, who ultimately lead Johnny to his
downfall by suggesting that the blacks are totally responsible for the
accumulation of debris. In his disturbed mind he confuses his personal
neurosis with the collective fear of his social class and transposes to
a social plane his unique pathological fixation:

> Toutes les rues sont en effet couvertes par les détritus que
> les noirs ne cessent d'y déposer. Et si je te disais qu'hier . . .

JOAN BROWN

> James et moi, nous soupçonnons un ouvrier de la fabrique . . . [9]

And it is finally the wife and the brother who benefit most, when
in spite of the court's endeavor to exonerate Johnny of the murder
of a black man, it is forced by the psychotic ravings of his final
outburst to send him back to a mental clinic. He is judged and condemned, however, not for his real crime, the premeditated murder
of Tom Guinness the Black, but because (1) he might someday be
capable of killing a white man and (2) he has failed to adapt to the
social and economic policies of his white society. The Avocat général
concludes:

> Il n'est pas besoin d'être psychiatre pour déclarer formelle-
> ment qu'un blanc prêt à tuer d'autres blancs sous le prétexte
> qu'un jour ceux-ci pourraient lui chercher querelle, qu'un tel
> homme est un malade, et même un malade dangereux. De
> plus, l'accusé a — ne l'oublions pas — déjà témoigné de son
> inadaption sociale, et je dirais même de tendances rétro-
> grades en refusant à maintes et maintes reprises de contri-
> buer avec les siens à l'essor commun, qui, exige une concen-
> tration toujours accrue de la production nationale. [10]

Moreover, the very trial-format itself reinforces and promotes the
social vision of racism under attack in the play. For the trial takes

---

[8] *La Politique des Restes*, p. 168.
[9] *La Politique des Restes*, p. 172.
[10] *La Politique des Restes*, p. 185.

place in a closed courtroom, no jury, no Blacks. It is a trial wherein the real accused, the Black Man, is totally excluded, his presence felt only by its intruding absence. He is talked about, victimized, mocked and feared, but he has no active role in the proceedings. This is white apartheid society's ultimate judgement of his disposability, of his "thingness," of the black as an article of commerce who, as Jacques Guicharnaud points out in his *Modern French Theater,* intimidates only when his numbers grow at an overwhelming rate:

> Without foundering in a demonstrative discourse, the play is a gripping metaphor of one vision of the modern world in which a proliferation of refuse and a proliferation of human beings leads to the same terror. [11]

He is a thing, a man-object, obliged by white society to be something other than what he is. His unique subjectivity is victimized for profit and vanity, deformed to fit an alien mold and ultimately mutilated beyond recognition.

But white society, the play demonstrates, must pay the price for this heinous crime. For the madness of Johnny Brown is only an extreme form of the fear that permeates this society, a final stage of the soul-sickness of a racist vision. In a society where man supresses others, he must eventually fear them. And in fearing them, he fears life. Life itself becomes hostile, each gesture of daily life a threat to his security, his sanity, his existence. It is only a matter of degree and limits in determining at what stage man's soul-sickness is psychotic, as Dr. Perkins points out in his diagnosis of Johnny:

> Ses interprétations délirantes ne connaissaient plus de bornes. Chaque geste de la vie quotidienne était interprété par lui comme hostile à son égard. [12]

The trial format of the play, while for the most part realistic, is combined with an intermittent series of flashbacks that dramatize on a raised podium the incidents leading up to the trial, sometimes supporting the evidence, sometimes contradicting it. The effect of psychic

---

[11] Jacques Guicharnaud in collaboration with June Guicharnaud, *Modern French Theatre from Giraudoux to Genet* (Revised ed.; New Haven and London, 1967), p. 202.

[12] *La Politique des Restes,* p. 156.

distancing is enhanced by having the characters in the courtroom drama leave their roles temporarily to cross to the podium and play themselves in the flashback scenes. The tension created by the contrast of past and present, truth and lie, fact and fiction, reality and madness accentuates the dramatic movement towards a gradual and then increasingly rapid disintegration of the play's racist universe. This disintegration of the accused and the society which he parallels is further propelled by the repetitious testimony of the series of witnesses, each in his own way testifying to the absence of sanity and human values in the play's universe, but with variation and increasing conclusiveness. Jimmy Madison the worker, Dr. Perkins the psychiatrist, Mr. Calao the barber, Joan Brown the wife, and James Brown the brother, intensify by their evidence against Johnny and by their collusion and complicity with the societal system our judgement of a world gone psychotic with fear.

Finally, however, it is Johnny himself who testifies best to his own madness when he defends his murder of Tom Guinness:

> Je ne pensais d'abord qu'à frapper Tom Guinness, mais lorsque je le vis à demi nu, avec ses pieds noirs, et la plante de ses pieds à demi blanche, je ne pus me contenir davantage. Du noir, du jaune, du blanc sur un même pied, c'est, il me semble, beaucoup. [13]

But if it is the psychotic ravings of Johnny's testimony which best convict him, it is the summation statement of the Avocat général that most convincingly inculpates the social system whose racism parallels Johnny's psychosis and of which the accused is both part and product:

> Il a tiré sur le noir Tom Guinness, se sentant ou se croyant menacé, mais aussi, mais surtout, effrayé par la prolifération sans cesse grandissante, il faut bien le reconnaître, des noirs dans notre État. ... mais il ne faut pas oublier non plus que cette nervosité, cet emportement, cet exercice illégitime, et j'y reviens, répréhensible, de la violence, lui ont été dictés essentiellement par le souci ombrageux, exagéré, et même dévoyé, je vous l'accorde, mais sincère, non seulement de

---

[13] *La Politique des Restes,* p. 175.

> ses propres intérêts et de ceux des siens, mais aussi des inté-
> rêts, légitimes, de notre État. [14]

Thus *La Politique des Restes* establishes Johnny's psychosis not
as an explanation of racism, but as a structure parallel to it, a metaphor of the soul-sickness prevalent in his society. The trial is, in
effect, a dramatization of a particular society's attempt to absolve
itself of the guilt and concomitant fear it knows as a result of the
degradation which its social system has brought to bear on others.

Time and language are two principal concerns of Adamov's theater
both in the early and later plays. But nowhere is the role of time
and especially language more central to the play's cohesiveness than
in *Sainte Europe*. As early as 1962, with the writing of the play
still in progress, Adamov described its purpose and the means whereby
he hoped to achieve that end:

> ... ce sera une caricature de notre monde, soyons précis,
> du monde dit "libre," du monde occidental ... Précisons.
> Qu'est-ce que je veux d'abord montrer dans *Sainte Europe*?
> Cet âge-ci, ou plus exactement, ce régime-ci dans cet âge-ci,
> qui se cache, se travestit sous les oripeaux d'un autre âge:
> à savoir le Moyen Age. Et cela pour en arriver à de petites
> fins sordides (bien sûr). [15]

The play is divided into two similar but unequally long parts. The
first five tableaux, comprising the *Première Partie*, describe the regime
of Karl of Franconia, its role in the Confédération Républicaine Nord-
Centre-Sud-Européenne, and its crusade against the atheistic Bolsheviks of the East. The *Deuxième Partie* with its two tableaux repeats
in general, but with the notable absence of Karl who has died, the
continued but disintegrating struggle of the privileged forces of society
against the suppressed classes both in Europe and the rising Third
World.

The seven tableaux of the play alternate "realistic" scenes (the
Agha, reactionary sovereign of the East, has come to the court of
Karl seeking financial and military support in their mutual struggles

---

[14] *La Politique des Restes,* p. 178.
[15] Arthur Adamov, *Ici et maintenant* (Paris, 1964), p. 177.

against the atheistic Bolsheviks) with dream sequences (three major figures are permitted a dream of vengeful accomplishment). The unifying factor which ties together these disparate elements of dream and reality within the crumbling empire is the need for the "dream" to go on, for the feast of power and pomp to perpetuate itself. The original reception must continue even though the drunken Agha's gift cannot arrive because of a strike. Ousanah, the Agha's wife, is quick to relieve herself of responsibility to her nation's earthquake victims by the gesture of adopting one small child.

If reality does not permit the "feast" to go on in the "realistic" scenes, then it continues in the private world of dream and fantasy. When the reality of the socio-political situation will not bend to Karl's will, he dreams of himself as the new Charlemagne just as Teresa avoids the ignominy and frustration of her husband Crépin's rejection in a dream of sainthood and sex with the Christ. When Honoré de Rubens, the powerful banker, is troubled by the irregularity of certain of his financial dealings, he is redeemed by a dream wherein he buys eternal salvation from the pope.

In spite of strikes, earthquakes, and political uprisings the masquerade persists throughout the play, the fiction of power and privilege alternately sustained by noble-sounding language, vengeful dreams, and masked balls until the inauthentic universe can no longer withstand the reality of revolution crushing in on it. Franconia and holy Europe, like Francesca and Moeller in the Epilogue, can no longer avoid the inescapable conclusion that the parody of holy empire, crusades to the East, and privileged classes that they are living must end so that authentic life can begin:

FRANCESCA

Dites, Moeller, croyez-vous que la vie changera, et pour de bon, une fois?

MOELLER

Ne le sais. Et puis le temps passe si vite, que tout cela vraiment. . . . [16]

---

[16] Arthur Adamov, *Sainte Europe* in *Théâtre III* (Paris, 1966), p. 286.

The gradual and then rapid disintegration of the play's universe is then demonstrated by a repetitive structure of intensification which restates with varying but increasingly powerful images the basic absence of authentic values characteristic of the world of *Sainte Europe*. By a series of parallel yet variant images the play exposes the basic underlying inauthenticity of Karl's vision as a parody of the middle ages, for while the language and symbols of medieval evangelism persist, the unifying spiritual dimension has been replaced by personal and selfish motives. The emptiness of Karl's dream of grandeur dominating the *Première Partie* with all its vanity, self-preservation and maintenance of privilege is structurally repeated and thematically reinforced by the empty self-serving political caution of Crépin in the *Deuxième Partie*. As power passes from Karl to Crépin and finally to Honoré the banker, the system's mask of noble enterprise is increasingly stripped of any vestigal images of virtue and authentic value as the corroding selfishness of the play's universe is exposed in its final stages of decadence and decomposition.

Karl's dream of Franconia and Europe rescuing the world from change dies with him at the end of the *Première Partie*. His successor Crépin buys time for himself and the system by consorting with Karl's former competitor, the Nord-Centre-Amérique. Honoré, representing the financial underpinnings of the system and revealed in the final tableau as the ultimate key to preserving the system, is finally exposed as being concerned only with saving his own soul. Thus Karl's final words at death, "Il est temps." [17] which end the *Première Partie* and signify that the time of Karl is over, are fulfilled by the final lines of the play chanted by the revolutionaries, "Liberté: Liberté: Il est temps!" [18] which signify that the time of inauthentic and suppressive social systems is at an end.

The play telescopes centuries of history within one epoch, the time of Karl, Crépin, Honoré and the Nord-Centre-Amérique, exposing the process of gradual disintegration and decomposition set in motion by the inner core of inauthenticity and selfishness inherent in its social and political systems. The "time" of the play is not really then limited to the time of Karl and the Nord-Centre-Amérique. For as indicated by the play's prologue wherein a direct temporal line is

---

[17] *Sainte Europe*, p. 257.
[18] *Sainte Europe*, p. 289.

established stretching from the Crusades to the present, man's subjugation of man is a continuing process and demands to be exposed
as the corrosive, deforming phenomenon that it is:

> On doit les marchands
> Desseur toutes gens honorer
> Quand ils font part terre et mer
> Et en maints estrangers pays
> Voyages pour quérir laine et vair et gris.
> Dieu garde les marchands du mal
> Que nous en amendons souvent.
> Sainte Eglise priemièrement
> Fut par marchands establie
> Et sachez que Chevalerie
> Doit aussi marchands tenir chers. [19]

The stilted, composite and inauthentic language of M. le Prologue
celebrating the merchant and the power of finance anticipates the
language of the play. The emptiness, the absence of truth and authenticity that characterizes the world of *Sainte Europe* is best revealed
by its language wherein old formulae, once vested with significance
and nobility, are used to shield the protagonists from the vacuity of
their situation. It is language of caricature which avoids or fails to
account for the reality of the situation in which it is used. Karl's
opening address as he receives the Agha is a masterpiece of denial
and illusion. It pretends to make of their sordid meeting — two selfish and weak leaders uniting in greed and self-preservation — something other than what it is:

> Nous, Karl, Empereur d'Occident ou, pour autres mots em-
> ployer, du Pays Franc et de l'Alémanie et de la Castille,
> Nous et notre fille, Grethe-France-Laure, et également notre
> Banquier Protégé Conseiller Aimé: Honoré de Rubens et
> derrière Nous enfin — je vous en prie, Agha — (Puis, à
> Ousannah Nanah, assez méprisant:) et vous, retournez-vous
> et voyez, pour vous — par Nous conviés, et partant présents
> dans le Miroir Un et Multiple de l'Histoire, tous les Sou-
> verains et Souveraines de notre lointain passé, perdu mais
> toujours, toujours retrouvé. Ou pour autres mots employer,
> Hildegarde et Frédegone et Sigismond et Tancrède et Lo-
> thaire, tous et toutes qui, comme Nous, sont soucieux, et

---

[19] *Sainte Europe*, p. 192.

heureux, d'accueillir en Aix-les-Chapelles et en vos personnes les représentants authentiques d'une dynastie qui, depuis toujours veilla et régna sur l'Iran, sur le Berceau de l'Histoire, partant. [20]

It is a language of lies, a language used to contradict reality by denouncing its authenticity. When the people in revolt justly cry out for their rightful freedoms, Innocent XXV comforts the agitated Agha by attributing misconception and self-deception to their legitimate needs:

> Oui, je les entends, Agha, et j'en suis attristé au plus profond de moi — même. Que ce saint mot de liberté soit proféré dans un sens différent de celui que lui attribuèrent les Pères de l'Eglise... Qui, attristé, pour eux comme pour nous tous. (Soupirant profondément.) O vies désunies! O chemins détournés! [21]

But mostly it is a language of self-contradiction, a language which gives the lie to itself by being understood simultaneously on two levels which contradict each other. It is a language where the tone negates the content or the gesture contradicts the words. When Pope Innocent entrusts Teresa with the task of creating holy places, she accepts the role but contradicts the very words themselves by her language of gesture, thereby revealing in the process a truth beyond the content of the words:

INNOCENT XXV, chantant:

> Qui en effet saurait désirer le Seigneur Sinon Toi, Teresa, alliant la Grâce et la Loi? (Cessant de chanter, et baisant les pieds de Teresa après l'avoir déchaussée, ce qui la fait glousser un peu.) Ma fille, je sais que tu n'as pu jusqu'ici te soutenir, étant pour ainsi dire absente de la Vie; mais ce monde demeure, mais si imparfait, si défectueux, qu'il faut, à tout prix, y créer de Saints Lieux. (Emphatique.) Mère Teresa, c'est (j'y reviens) toi qui les instaurera. (Très homme d'affaires.) Je t'en donnerai les moyens.
> (Innocent XXV tend les billets de banque à Teresa qui, imitant les putains du temps de Toulouse-Lautrec, les enfile, promptement, dans ses bas.) [22]

---

[20] *Sainte Europe,* pp. 193-94.
[21] *Sainte Europe,* p. 277.
[22] *Sainte Europe,* p. 240.

The progressive deterioration of the vision and mission of these descendants of the crusades is best shown by the inauthenticity of their language, which while using the images and symbols of the past, is devoid of its spiritual dimension. This language of imposture betrays, reflects and promotes at the same time the ethical bankruptcy of those modern social, political and economic systems that debase and degrade man, sacrificing him to an ideology and manipulating him as an object of trade.

Adamov creates in this play a purely theatrical language whose various tones and levels contradict each other and expose the basic emptiness or inauthenticity of the play's universe. This stress on the tension between language and language as the dominant figure of exposure and revelation makes of *Sainte Europe* an excellent example of what Champigny means by "un théâtre du langage":

> Le théâtre contemporain est un théâtre du langage plutôt qu'un langage de personnages. La tension entre langage et langage y est la figure dominante, en particulier sous la forme que nous avons appelée "verticale." (J'entends par là une tension qui s'exerce entre dramatique et non dramatique, ou entre des niveaux de dramatisation.) [23]

This "created" composite language of *Sainte Europe* frees the play from the limitations of time and space established by the geographical locations and temporal sequences of the story. It achieves for the play its own "time" and "space." As Henri Gouhier points out in *Le Théâtre et L'Existence*:

> Chaque drame a son espace et son temps: ils ne sont pas cadres extérieurs à l'action comme l'espace des bornes kilométriques et le temps des horloges: c'est l'action elle-même qui, en se dilatant, engendre son espace d'une géographie plus ou moins poétique et son temps lourd d'histoires plus ou moins légendaires. [24]

The world of *Sainte Europe* is the world of inauthenticity of which modern man is the ultimate victim. The play calls attention to the absence of significant human values that characterizes the modern epoch as revealed by the emptiness and deceit of its language.

---

[23] Robert Champigny, *Le Genre dramatique* (Monte-Carlo, 1965), p. 176.
[24] Henri Gouhier, *Le Théâtre et L'Existence* (Paris, 1952), p. 29.

This degradation of language is, as Adamov had pointed out some twenty years earlier in *L'Aveu,* the visible and infallible sign of man's corruption:

> La dégradation du langage est le signe visible, infaillible, du mal. Chaque jour, les noms que l'homme jadis proférait avec vénération et selon l'ordre, sont astreints aux pires contrefaçons du sens. Presque à coup sûr l'homme clairvoyant peut dénoncer l'indignité de tout ce qui apparaît vêtu des noms les plus hauts. Car cette vêture n'est qu'un mensonge, le voile de l'usurpation. C'est le masque d'or qui recouvre la lèpre de l'innommable sans face. [25]

M. le Modéré is the most obviously humorous of Adamov's plays. It brings to the surface the persistent laugh that confronts the tragic and the absurd throughout his theater. Adamov himself called the play a "clownerie" and recognized in its exaggeration and caricature a return to his earlier approach:

> *M. le Modéré,* à présent. Toute la pièce doit être une clownerie. Que les gestes eux-mêmes soient outrés, caricaturaux. Retour à l'absurde d'une certaine manière. [26]

While the play is relatively short, it is divided into three parts with twenty-three tableaux and a prologue, no scene being more than a few minutes in duration. The continual rising and falling of the curtain adds a dimension of repetition and caricature to this already tragi-comic series of adventures which describes the rise and fall of a man of moderation who pushes moderation in all his affairs to an extreme and thereby denies the poetry, imagination and validity of life.

The nine tableaux of the *Première Partie* take place in Paris, where M. le Modéré, his wife Clo, and his daughter Mado open the Hôtel des Quatre Saisons. While insistent that everything be in its proper order and proportion, M. le Modéré succeeds in hiring a homosexual-voyeur as manager, beats up his wife over a minor dispute, permits his daughter a lesbian friendship with another tenant, is drawn into an incestuous and homosexual relationship with his daughter and

---

[25] *L'Aveu,* p. 108.
[26] Arthur Adamov, *L'Homme et L'Enfant* (Paris, 1968), p. 231.

her friend, and finally plays out a familiar drama of sexual perversion with his wife. Having proved his talent at organizing and administering a hotel, he is chosen by M. Havas, one of the three or four astute politicians assigned by the Americans to direct the destiny of Europe, to represent the Party of Moderation in his native Jura.

It is a world wherein the absurd is accepted as the norm, where pattern and repetition, no matter how ridiculous, establish the terms of existence. When in the second tableau Clo becomes delirious after being knocked down by her husband, M. le Modéré regulates for his hotel manager the apparent disorder by replacing it in its context:

M. LE MODÉRÉ

Ne vous en faites pas pour elle. Elle délire ainsi à peu près tous les mercredis. (Inquiet:) On est bien mercredi, aujourd'hui?

M. WILLIAM

Oui.

M. LE MODÉRÉ

Alors, tout est dans l'ordre. [27]

The second part continues M. le Modéré's dizzying ascent to power. Throughout most of the act he is the Chief of the State of Jura, attempting to lead his people down a path of moderation avoiding the excesses of both revolutionaries and reactionaries. And yet he repeats in this new context excesses of moderation parallel to the follies of the opening section. The average or mediocre advisers that he chooses are too mediocre and fail him. The moderate punishment that he metes out to the striking workers in his state is not enough to dissuade them and too much to convert them. Thus he is overthrown by his Chief of Police who judges him guilty of excessive moderation:

Quoi, ton papa? Il exagérait, ton papa, voilà tout. On a beau être du Parti des Modérés, il y a quand même des moments historiques où il faut forcer un peu la note, non? [28]

---

[27] Arthur Adamov, *M. le Modéré* in *Théâtre IV* (Paris, 1968), p. 24.
[28] *M. le Modéré*, p. 58.

Brought to power by a political party of moderation in a social system that shuns reactionary and revolutionary approaches, M. le Modéré is exiled for his unimaginative adherence to the party's principles. The play depicts the tragedy of modern man's subjectivity, sensitivity, individuality and imagination being mutilated by a false concept of reality inherited from the very socio-political system of which he is a part. And as in *Sainte Europe* it is the language, or the degradation of the language, which best reveals this disintegrating process.

In the third and final part of the play, the interior or psycho-spiritual mutilation of M. le Modéré is represented literally by his physical invalidism — he is confined to a wheelchair and is dependent on his daughter and his wife — as well as by his geographical exile in London. He has become an alcoholic who drinks to forget and who believes it possible to "moderate" his drinking:

> Tu as raison. Il faut absolument que je me contrôle. (Il redresse son bar, se remet sur son tabouret, boit deux verres l'un sur l'autre, puis, rabattant bar et tabouret, disparaît dans sa voiture:) Oui, oui, que je me contrôle, et que je ne prenne pas à jeun plus de dix à douze bières allemandes, danoises, néerlandaises, qu'importe; et deux à ... quatre gins, et c'est tout. [29]

Blinded by his alcoholism, a final manifestation of his total and irrevocable psycho-physical deterioration, and prompted by reasons of political and social expediency, M. le Modéré permits his daughter to marry le Prince de Galles, a homosexual who involves her in his perverse preoccupations.

Victimized by the capriciousness of his family, the unimaginativeness of his political party, the inauthenticity of his society and ultimately by his own spiritual bankruptcy, M. le Modéré is reduced by his physical paralysis and geographical confinement to a total and literal dependence on the very people and the very system that destroyed him. Thus the play demonstrates by the most simple and literal of images the precariousness of the human condition to which man in his powerlessness is subject.

---

[29] *M. le Modéré*, p. 77.

The cogency of the play's statement is due largely to a return to that type of "literal" theater that dominated Adamov's early work and which succeeded, as Jean Duvignaud points out in his *Sociologie du Théâtre,* in awakening and provoking man's latent energy:

> En ce sens, le théâtre de la littéralité, qui présente la personne humaine dans sa nudité et recourt aux éléments les plus simples pour en démontrer la situation périlleuse, exerce une fonction salutaire et libératoire. Au lieu de consoler l'homme, de l'endormir par des paroles et des sentiments, il l'éveille et le provoque. Il cherche à exciter chez lui une energie latente qui est une forme de la liberté collective. [30]

The M. le Modéré who exposes his refusal of choice and commitment in the apparently harmless terms of the *Prologue* is subject, because of this very fear to honestly engage life, to a continuing series of debilitating adventures which finally ends in his total physical, psychological and spiritual disintegration. From tableau to tableau the pattern is repeated with only slight variation of circumstances but with a mounting intensity as M. le Modéré submits to continual assaults on his individuality and subjectivity. The spiritual bankruptcy of his psychotic commitment to moderation permits his integrity and unity to be repeatedly violated by circumstance, ambition, his daughter, her friends, his political associates, and alcohol until he is reduced to a state of helpless dependency on others. The prevailing absence of faith in life which characterizes M. le Modéré makes him the ultimate reflection of a society, a socio-political system that fears most of all the ascendancy to power of the imagination. He is the designated victim of a logic which in seeking not to do much invariably leads to the worst excesses. Thus the power and ironic humor of the play rests, as Jacques Lemarchand points out, on the simple revelation that the absence of commitment to values is in reality the most dangerous of self-deceptions:

> Et la pièce prend tout son sens, et sa force comique, dans le fait devenu éclatant que la modération pousée à l'extrême est le pire débauche de l'imagination. [31]

---

[30] Jean Duvignaud, *Sociologie du Théâtre* (Paris, 1965), p. 550.

[31] Jacques Lemarchand, "*M. le Modéré* d'Arthur Adamov," *Le Figaro littéraire* (7-13 oct. 1968), p. 39.

Moreover, M. le Modéré's failure to accept reality on its own terms, his need to compromise the forces of life because of fear, is demonstrated most dramatically by the language in which he seeks to shelter himself. He becomes paralyzed, immobilised by his dominating need to allow for all contingencies. He becomes a prisoner of the possible, incapable of resisting infinite projection even when asking his hotel manager to perform the simple if ludicrous task of carrying his daughter up to her girlfriend's room:

> Mlle Liehn demeure, je crois bien, à l'entresol. Et l'entresol n'est pas, n'est-ce pas, un étage supérieur. Encore qu'en se jetant de l'entresol au sol, on puisse très bien se casser les côtes, ou un bras, ou deux bras, ou même, bien que cela semble quelque peu abusif, excessif en un mot — on peut très bien, pourquoi se dérober, se le dissimuler, se casser un bras et deux jambes, pour ne citer qu'un exemple, entre... beaucoup d'autres. [32]

It is a language that reveals to us the crumbling unity of his being, the disintegration in progress, while at the same time it serves to protect him from the fear and doubt that plague him and of which he is aware in the opening tableau:

> Mon malheur, vois-tu, c'est le doute. Ainsi, je me dis: d'une part, Clo a raison, et d'autre part: Clo se trompe. Oh, ces oscillations, bien trop vives, bien trop excessives! (Bas:) Si encore j'aboutissais quelque part! [33]

But it is also a language which is humorous. It is a grotesque, exaggerated language of caricature that reflects a society which parodies life, a socio-economic system which rather than go to the root of a problem, seeks to balance the problem out of existence. And M. le Modéré is the ultimate development of this system, a father who rather than discourage or prohibit his daughter from wearing excessively short skirts, attempts to re-establish equilibrium by adding a long dress to her collection:

> Écoute-moi bien... Tu vas ouvrir l'armoire, et là, au milieu des robes courtes de Mado — je dis courtes pour ne pas dire

---

[32] *M. le Modéré*, p. 28.
[33] *M. le Modéré*, p. 20.

davantage —, tu en trouveras une belle, brune et longue, une robe que j'ai mise là parmi les petites jupes de la fillette pour que l'équilibre soit ... soit rétabli. Tu comprends? (Grave:) Il avait besoin de l'être. [34]

M. le Modéré is a man of the times, the time of personal and collective ignominy. His journey of personal disintegration from Paris to the Jura to London is a metaphor of modern man's journey away from reality towards the inaction and sterility of fantasy. The play's power resides in its concrete image of the futility of evasion. It holds up to ridicule and laughter the politics of moderation and compromise, exposing as comic the self-delusions to which we are subject. Its humor, as Jacques Lemarchand suggests, is ferocious and painful, but it is also man's last defense against the absurdity of his own socio-political systems:

> Ce rire, d'ailleurs, et contrairement à une idée généralement reçue, soustend à peu près tout le théâtre d'Adamov. C'est le rire de la caricature, un rire assez féroce, un rire qui fait parfois mal; et ici, pour la première fois, il se veut et se fait franc rire. Mais cette ironie, cette affirmation presque burlesque de l'imbécillité et de la méchanceté, il était possible de les déceler dès les premières pièces de l'auteur de *Paolo Paoli*; cette *Parodie*, cette *Invasion*, qu'il n'a pas du tout raison de renier. [35]

But it is *Off Limits* that is the fullest expression of his vision of the contemporary world and its systems as the "temps de l'ignominie." By using an America sick with imperialistic war and inner conflicts revealed by racism and abuse of drugs as the setting for his play, Adamov succeeds in describing the anguish of a modern society in crisis and its paralyzing effects on a cross section of the people making up and perpetuating that society.

The play is not anti-American in any simplistic sense, but rather it recognizes America and its socio-political systems as an extreme example of a life lived without recourse to the spiritual dimension. It is an America which Adamov considered, as reported in an interview with Nicole Zand, as the most probing example of the malaise and

---

[34] *M. le Modéré*, p. 34.
[35] Lemarchand, p. 38.

antagonisms of contemporary society in general, which he felt to be in its final stages of disintegration:

> L'Amérique est importante dans la mesure où elle est au fond ce que nous sommes en le poussant plus loin, en le poussant "off limits." On retrouve là-bas, exacerbés, touts les antagonismes de notre société contemporaine: entre l'amour et l'érotisme, entre le désir de paix et le besoin d'action, entre le désir de connaissance et le mépris de toute connaissance, entre le besoin de fraternité et la haine presque physique de ce qui n'est pas américain de longue date. Tous les antagonismes . . . [36]

The play is divided into five tableaux and an epilogue. Each tableau represents a party or reception; each tableau repeats with slight variations and increasing intensity the empty frenzy of a group of New York intellectuals, media people, and young drug addicts bent on self-destruction. Whatever revolt they can muster against the established order, with its vacuity, degradation and oppressive war in Vietnam, is smothered by their self-pity, vanity, selfishness, eroticism and alcoholism. Their flirtations, drunken accusations, staged "happenings," petty conceits and enmities vary little from party to party, revealing each participant to be both a victim and perpetrator of a destructive social order which permits only the illusion of escape. The momentary release of their pent-up aggressiveness and frustrated anguish at drunken parties makes them only more aware of their incapacity to act, to break with the system.

It is this very monotony of ineffectual masochism and the repetitiousness of meaningless escapism throughout the first four tableaux or parties that finally convince the young lover-addicts Jim and Sally to act. Their growth up and away from the debilitating cycle of parties and drugs, their eventual deaths in a gesture of defiance and revolt against the system, and the system's ironic triumph by absorbing their defiance and capitalizing on it form the central drama of the play.

Jim and Sally represent a threat to the noisy chaos and changing hostilities that dominate the drunken parties of the first four tableaux.

---

[36] Nicole Zand, "Entretien avec Arthur Adamov," *Le Monde* (24 janv. 1969), p. 13

They embody the two constants which are the nuclei of individual and societal redemption: (1) the genuine love they feel for each other, and (2) their intense hatred of the oppressive war in Vietnam.

It is a love which first begins as an erotic fascination. In Tableau I at the first party of the television magnate Humphrey, Sally and Jim speak of its irregular beginnings:

SALLY

C'est mon obstination qui t'a séduit?

JIM

Oui, sans parler de la frimousse, bien sûr.

SALLY

Et aussi parce que tu m'avais vue faire la putain à Central Park, avoue?

JIM

Oui, aussi. Parce qu'à cette époque-là vois-tu, je n'avais jamais encore couché avec une putain. [37]

But in contrast to the decaying world around them, their love flowers and grows in intensity from tableau to tableau. When by the fourth party Sally has convinced Jim that their only redemption lies in escape from the life they are leading, their devotion to each other's well-being is complete and even obvious to others. At the end of the fourth tableau in the closing *Récitatif* — one of a series of self-critical free-verse forms that punctuate the play and comment on its action — Molly, alone on stage and facing the audience, celebrates their union and its healing power:

> Sally Jim pense à toi Il pense à toi toujours
> Et je ne sais pas ce que vous ferez tous les
>   deux ensemble
> Vous vous disputerez souvent encore je suppose
> Mais je sais que Jim t'aime Sally
> Et qu'il ira
> N'importe où

[37] Arthur Adamov, *Off Limits* (Paris, 1969), p. 51.

En taule Dans un hôpital psychiatrique Ailleurs
Là où tu seras Il te rejoindra

Dis Sally s'ils tuaient ton Jim Tu pleurerais. [38]

In a parallel fashion Jim and Sally's hatred of the Vietnam War, which takes the form of ineffectual mockery in the opening tableau, grows in intensity and meaningful direction as the play progresses. The empty play-acting of the first tableau begins to take on substance as the relationship between the war and the insane behavior of the party-goers becomes more evident. James Andrews, a young British journalist in New York to study the "drug culture," is forced to conclude in the closing *Récitatif* of Tableau II:

Humanisme
Il m'a fallu du temps beaucoup de temps pour apprendre
que la ligne de la vie passe par le Vietnam
Et que si le Président Johnson n'est pas traduit devant un
tribunal révolutionnaire
Tu ne pourrais plus Jim te promener paisible à demi mort
dans Washington Square
La police ne s'occupera même pas de toi
Trop à faire par ailleurs. [39]

It is in Tableau III when Jim tears up his draft card that he commits his first punishable act, his first real and meaningful act of revolt. When Sally convinces him in Tableau IV that they must flee New York and America if they are to save their integrity and sanity, he exposes himself to arrest and death. It is at this point that the two constants of love for each other and mutual hatred for the war which have grown in depth and intensity from tableau to tableau coalesce and permit the couple to break forth from the vicious cycle of meaningless existence in New York. The unity of the first four tableaux resides in the very growth and action of the young couple and their ultimate reaction to both the stupidity and oppressiveness of the war and the senseless repetition of parties and drugs.

Although Jim and Sally die at the Mexican border, he without his passport in resisting arrest, she in a sympathetic death of revolt, the

---

[38] *Off Limits,* p. 135.
[39] *Off Limits,* p. 81.

5ᵉTableau or "seconde party chez Humphrey" is in a sense an extension of or reaction to the young couple's drama of defiance and death. It represents the very real need of the others for the "eternal Party" to go on, to try once again as in the preceding four tableaux to escape the reality of their lives, to mollify their conscience and ease the pain of their guilt. Even with Jim and Sally dead, the presence in death of the young couple is felt as a threat to the others and the need for the comedy of farce of life lived with illusions to go on is now even more desperate:

GEORGE

Faire quoi? Elle (Sally) ne voulait ni de toi, ni de moi, ne de rien. Elle n'en pouvait plus de jouer la comédie.

DOROTHY, (*ironique*)

Nous la jouons bien encore, toi et moi.

GEORGE, (*très triste*)

Oui, nous la jouons encore, toi et moi. [40]

But the usual frenetic round of drinking, happenings and drugs fails to silence the guilt and shame they all feel in varying degrees. The senselessness and futility of their lives has been exposed and challenged by the young couple's revolt against the debilitating system and the system must retaliate.

Thus the final tableau of the play, its epilogue, is an apparent break with the pattern of the preceding acts. It is the same group of empty people — Humphrey, Dorothy, Reynold Days, Doris Roan, etc. — but instead of coming together for one more party of an endless series, they unite in a final effort to nullify or obviate the seriousness of Jim and Sally's death by turning it into a harmless, romantic love story for television. By rendering inoffensive the death of the young couple and their ultimate rejection of the "American way of life," they seek to permit themselves to continue their own life of illusions as well as permit the system to devour others so that they might be preserved.

---

[40] *Off Limits,* p. 144.

146 THE THEATER OF ARTHUR ADAMOV

Thus while the closing tableau varies from the cycle of repetitive parties, it extends from it and is necessary for such a way of life to go on, for the eternal party of selfishness, inauthenticity and oppression to continue. As B. Poirot-Delpech points out in a review of the play, the epilogue depicts the power of the system to recuperate and turn to its advantage even the very act of revolt against the system:

> L'épilogue de la pièce démonte, précisément, ce processus de travestissement grâce auquel la société américaine récupère à son profit tout ce qui la menace. Avant de payer son mensonge d'un infarctus — lui-même maquillé en héroïsme — le producteur ami des deux enfants change leur contestation brouillonne mais dérangeante en une superbe et inoffensive histoire d'amour. Cette fin ne tranche qu'en apparence avec les tableaux précédents. [41]

The endless round of senseless parties is brought to a halt, at least within the play, by the death of the young couple Sally and Jim. The five parties that make up the first five tableaux are variations of each other, each tableau divided into scenes taking place in the *vestiaire,* the *grande salle,* or the *couloir* of someone's home, the Humphrey's, the Watkins', Doris Roan's. Each tableau represents a party almost exactly like the one the night before, with the same drunken, vicious people, the same pile of coats. The parties are filled with the same bizarre mixture of political bickering, staged happenings, and bitter recriminations. No one party is any better or any worse than the others.

It is rather the accumulation by repetition of selfish and senseless behavior throughout the first four tableaux that accentuates the differences between Jim and Sally and the others and ultimately provokes the young couple's flight. The structure of *Off Limits* is one of gradual and then rapid disintegration of the play's universe by the intensification by repetition of the prevailing inauthenticity of values. The sterility, impotency and puerile revolts of the "chic" New York intellectuals exhibited in the first four tableaux contrast sharply with the young couple's genuine love for each other and mutual hatred for the oppression of war. Ultimately these contrasts drive Jim and Sally to their act of defiance and death.

---

[41] B. Poirot-Delpech, "*Off Limits* d'Arthur Adamov," *Le Monde* (6 fév. 1969), p. 8.

The play's universe further disintegrates in the fifth tableau after the death of the young couple, when the second party at Humphrey's fails to have its usual narcotic effect, fails to dull the minds of the participants and erase Jim and Sally's repudiation of a life to which the others have grown accustomed. Thus they are driven to the final desperation of the Epilogue, an attempt to create for television a false but harmless drama out of defiance and death, to confiscate by falsification an authentic act of revolt.

This final gesture of inauthenticity, this final act of human betrayal, this testament to the degradation and disintegration of the system is not, however, without further deteriorating consequences, as George and Dorothy suffer the results of their complicity. Dorothy, who plays Sally in the televised broadcast, is brought to a new awareness of her own ineffectual reality and the debilitating lie to which she gives support so that the system might maintain its momentum. Plagued with guilt, fear and remorse she invokes Sally and asks her pardon in the final *Récitatif* of the play:

> Sally toi qui ne reviendras jamais jamais pardon
> Nous t'avons tous démentie neutralisée Cadavre maquillé
> Dorothy l'Anesthésiée a pris la place de la petite vivante
> morte [42]

Thus while the play depicts a social system capable of recuperating to its own advantage the disruptive elements of revolt and death, it also shows the great price the people who accept the system must pay.

Off Limits combines, although in a less integrated fashion than *Le Ping-Pong*, the two dominant directions of Adamov's dramaturgy, the theater of dream, neurosis and futility and the Brechtian theater of realistic social criticism. While the play is principally concerned with the social systems of alienated modern society and their resultant oppressive war, it unites and integrates the personal or individual dramas of Jim and Sally, George and Dorothy, Humphrey and Lisbeth and the others within the general destructive socio-political fabric. Personal neurosis and societal malaise, escapism and war, drugs and racism intermingle to create a nightmarish world.

---

[42] *Off Limits*, p. 170.

The play is more than a simple reportage. Not only does it succeed in portraying the inauthentic way of life as lived according to the ethic of evasion and rationalization, but it projects the very vertigo and confusion felt by the characters themselves. By the use of certain avant-garde techniques — *images fixes*, staged happenings, transitions between tableaux, self-critical *Récitatifs* in free verse form, symbolic décor, etc. — the play recreates the chaotic nightmare that it seeks to criticize.

Off Limits remains consistent with the basic thrust of Adamov's theater. It is a dramatic demonstration of the dominant theme of man using man as an object, or what Guicharnaud calls the "theme of the man-object":

> The theme of the man-object is the second constant in Adamov's works. Once again his point of departure is an existential anguish typical of the theatre of the fifties. More expressionistic or Germanic in form than Ionesco's or Beckett's, his plays point up the tragedy of conscious and irreplaceable subjectivity being incomprehensibly massacred, humiliated, or mutilated by the world. [43]

When Jim and Sally are reported dead, the others are principally concerned with the effect the death will have on their own lives. Having helped to drive the young couple to revolt and destruction, Humphrey and the others are now eager to capitalize on their death just as they had used them in life. Each in his own way will try to turn Jim and Sally's death to his own advantage. Humphrey, the media magnate, enlists the help of George, the writer, to convert the tragedy of revolt into a harmless television spectacle on love, youth and drugs:

> Non. Car je sais ce que tu vas me dire, que tu ne seras qu'un instrument entre mes mains, que tu écriras sous ma dictée, etc. etc. Eh bien, ce n'est pas vrai, j'ai besoin de toi, George. D'abord, bien sûr, parce que tu les as connus, toi, ces gamins, mieux que personne, peut-être, mais aussi parce que cette émission doit faire un boum, et que toi seul, avec ton langage, ton emportement d'écervelé, et les levées et tes retombées, peux permettre ce boum. Saisi? [44]

[43] Guicharnaud, p. 202.
[44] *Off Limits,* p. 145.

Off Limits depicts and condemns the social system of alienated modern society in America, its viciousness, perversion, degradation and inauthenticity. As in the other plays of this final phase of Adamov's theater, the accent is placed here on the absence of man's awareness of and concern for his fellow men as they live together in society. Moreover Adamov reconciles not only the thematic duality of "absurdist" and "political" orientations, but the formal divergencies of "avant-garde" and epic-realist dramaturgy. He moves towards a synthesis of form and content, a union of style and view that is particularly his own, that takes into account both man in the universe and man in society.

Having exposed America in *Off Limits* as the ultimate expression of contemporary emptiness and inauthenticity, Adamov in his final play *Si l'été revenait* (1970), reveals as false the "new myths" of a liberated, socialist Sweden. At the very beginning of the play a large placard bearing the image of a girl in a bathing suit descends onto an empty stage. A voice, speaking into a microphone, announces:

> Pourquoi sourit cette jolie fille? Parce qu'elle habite un pays où l'on ignore le chômage et la faim, où le crime est partiquement inexistant, où il n'y a ni taudis ni ghettos, où la guerre est inconnue depuis cent cinquante ans. [45]

What follows, however, is perhaps Adamov's most desperate image of modern man lost in a maze of selfishness, frustration, guilt, fear and impotency. Having failed to create an authentic unifying myth to fill the void of their existence, the characters of *Si l'été revenait* are reduced to performing in a dream world that is not always of their own making. It is Adamov's ultimate statement on absence, for in this play the absence of a spiritual dimension leads directly to the absence of life itself. There is no exit save dream or suicide.

Moreover, like the penultimate *Off Limits*, Adamov's final play depicts a world where socio-political action is continually stifled by the self-pity, vanity, selfishness, eroticism and masochism of its characters. And as in the other plays of this final cycle the accent in *Si l'été revenait* shifts from the political to the social, specifically to the failure of its characters to maintain the coherent and cooperative

---

[45] Arthur Adamov, *Si l'été revenait* (Paris, 1970), p. 15.

interdependence necessary for their survival. The play is a study in complex relationships threatened at their core by the characters' sado-masochism and guilt, by their inability to deal with ambivalent emotions of love and hate, dependence and dominance, faith and fear, gratitude and scorn, devotion and resentment. The play is primarily a psychological exposition, but unlike the archetypes of the early plays, the characters of *Si l'été revenait* are "realistic," living out their dreams in the specific context of contemporary Sweden. Thus, in its concern for the individual as well as for man's failure to build together as a social unit, *Si l'été revenait* comes full cycle and bears witness to the consistency of Adamov's theater.

The play does not so much tell or develop a story as it reveals in dream-sequences four different understandings of the same drama. The four story-tellers or dreamers — Lars, Thea, Brit and Alma — are united by a complex set of dependencies structured principally on eroticism, self-pity and guilt. Lars is having an incestuous affair with his sister Thea. She in turn resents his new wife Brit. Alma, who has contrived Lars' marriage to demonstrate her fancied superiority, enjoys erotic relationships with both the husband and the wife.

The other major participants in the dream-sequences — Mme Petersen, the familiar mother-castration figure of the early plays, Viktor, the older, more experienced friend who both attracts and influences Lars, and the Rector of the School of Medicine, the traditional symbol of authority — do not dream, but merely figure in the fantasies of the four principals. At the time the dreams begin Lars has been expelled from medical school, the last of a series of failures reminiscent of Professor Taranne, Thea is dead by suicide, blaming herself and her affair with her brother for the death of their mother, and Alma, frustrated at her inability to resolve socio-political problems in the Third World, has committed suicide. This is the stuff or material with which the four dreamers fashion the varying sequences which make up the play.

Lars dreams first, in the longest and most detailed dream-sequence, which introduces the complex set of relationships that dominate the play, the ambivalent feelings of the participants toward each other, and the prevailing mood of guilt and fear which pervades the play. With Lars in control of the fantasy the characters play out scenes from the past — Lars' first meeting with Brit, his dismissal from the School of Medicine. These moments from the past are freely mingled with scenes of the dream-present — Lars' insistence on his power to assure security not only to his wife but to all the women in the play, his refusal to accept responsibility for his sister's suicide, his struggle with guilt feelings over the death of Alma. The sequence ends with a pathetic and final cry for his lost sister.

The following sequences are variations of the same drama but from different perspectives. Thus in Thea's dream Lars' marriage to Brit is accompanied by his promise not to leave home, not to end their incestuous relationship. And while her view of the proceedings are dominated by feelings of guilt, her principal attitude is one of self-pity and a sense of exclusion. Her death by suicide is intimated in the closing image of her dream-sequence when she cries out:

> Et moi! Que fais-tu de moi, encore vivante! Vous m'en voulez peut-être parce que j'ai décidé de me tuer. Alma, Brit, Lars, vous, tous les trois, seuls. Et moi, seule, exclue, exclue! [46]

For Brit, Lars' failures and the multiple suicides serve as the material with which to fashion a drama of self-justification. Subject to Thea's antagonisms upon entering their home, forced to play out erotic scenes wherein she assumes the identity of the sister-lover, manipulated by and dependent on the dominating Alma, Brit in her fantasy views herself as the redeeming force in Lars' life. It is she who will save him from guilt. She has the power to make him "innocent." Together life will be possible.

> Dire qu'il va falloir vivre, et qu'on finira par la trouver normale, cette vie fichée entre deux morts.... Tu réussiras tes études d'architecte, Lars, et moi, grâce à toi, je serai maîtresse d'école, j'apprendrai l'arithmétique aux tout petits. Nous ne serons pas joyeux, oh non, mais tout de même heureux de vivre ensemble, de voir ensemble les jours s'enfuir. [47]

The "reality" of Alma's fantasy, the last of the four dreams, is shaped by a curious and contradictory combination of revolutionary zeal and sexual sadism, a desire for social justice and an overwhelming

---

[46] *Si l'été revenait,* p. 55.
[47] *Si l'été revenait,* p. 66.

sense of superiority. This complex androgynous beauty, who like Thea is already dead as her dream-sequence begins, looks upon Lars and Brit as inferiors, and this, to some extent, explains her attraction for them and her control over them. She arranges their marriage, delivering Brit, the object, to Lars, the former lover, in order to demonstrate her vaunted superiority, for in truth she recognizes herself as Lars' favorite, the preferred one. And just as she tries to dominate the personal affairs of Lars and Brit, so also does her complex set of motives drive her to engage in socio-political action in the Third World. When this fails, due largely to her own sado-masochistic neuroses, she commits suicide. The closing image of the play — Alma pushing Lars, Brit and Thea on the swing — introduces the final fusion of personal and political motifs. When Lars refers to Brit as the little third world which Alma has brought him, Alma begins to push the swing so violently that Thea falls off (her suicide). The force of the swing, however, also knocks Alma to the ground (her suicide). The ride on the swing is finally over. Only Lars and Brit remain. He embraces her and says, "Enfin, tout est réglé." [48]

The four dream-sequences, simultaneously consistent with, yet contradictory to, each other are like four images superimposed which hint at a truth far beyond the individual "truths" of each dreamer. They are variations on a same theme in a play which posits no objective version other than the play itself. Each new variation permits us to grow increasingly aware of the complex motives behind each human act, of the numerous possible interpretations, and finally of the elusiveness of reality itself.

The play's repetitive structure of intensification builds by accretion toward a composite image far more revealing and substantial than the individual interpretations of the separate sequences. Each dream repeats with variation the "facts" of the other dreams, intensifying by contrast the complicated drama of individuals who fail to harmonize. Rather than develop its story by progression, *Si l'été revenait* reveals by repetition with variation the failure of a small group of people to reach out and save each other and thereby save themselves.

Si l'été revenait is a play about absence. In an advanced socialist country where there is no hunger and practically no crime, man still

---

fails to bridge the gap between himself and others. The "new myths" of the "smiling girl in a bathing suit" are hollow and fail to create the unifying dimension necessary to fill the void in a world of absence, absence of communication, absence of innocence, and especially absence of man's awareness of and concern for his fellow man. Even the overt socio-political commitment of Alma ends in failure, a victim of her own pseudo-superiority as well as the callousness of the system itself.

The very title of the play intimates a lost or "absent" summer, a nostalgic longing for a unity that once was but is forever gone. The central image of the play, a recurrent motif of various principal characters riding a swing together while others push, represents a cohesive solidarity no longer attainable because the characters are incapable of cooperating to keep the swing going. It is the failure of the play's participants to maintain the coherent interdependence necessary for their very survival. In the "post-summer" days which make up the time of the play, there is no recourse but to dream (Lars and Brit), or to die (Thea and Alma). Other people — Mme Petersen, Viktor, the Rector — can do little else but witness the frustration of modern man spiritually bankrupt, floundering in contradiction, impotent when alone, and yet incapable of reaching out to save others and thereby save himself.

Central to this prevailing mood of impotency is a corrosive guilt and its concomitant fear which undermine the structure of the play's universe. Specific causes for this guilt abound throughout the play. Lars feels guilty for never having totally escaped from his mother's domination, for his failure to grow up and be a man. His repeated fiascos in chosen professions, his incestuous relationship with his sister, and especially the suicide-deaths of Thea and Alma all serve to heighten his sense of guilt. Thea, on the other hand, experiences guilt not only for the affair itself, but also for neglecting their mother and thereby causing her death. But the principal guilt of this play is a guilt that goes beyong specific cause. It is inherent in the very definition of the characters themselves, people at a loss to explain their very existence, people who rather than live prefer to dream or to die. It is a guilt they are incapable of explaining, but which pervades the very texture of their being. In Brit's self-justificatory dream Lars tells Viktor:

Car avoue que malgré tout tu te sens coupable, toi. Avoue que tu as fait quelque chose, je ne sais pas quoi, mais quelque chose, pour être ainsi pourchassé jour après jour. (Criant:) Rien n'est gratuit! Si je suis heureux, c'est parce que je me sens innocent. (Désignant Brit:) Innocenté par elle! [49]

Si l'été revenait is a fitting end-piece to a collection of plays that fused, better than any other contemporary theater, the divergent trends of French drama in the 1950's and 1960's. By mixing realism with fantasy, by superimposing variant dream-sequences for which there is no objective version, the play creates a world where psychological and socio-political elements coalesce into a highly theatrical language of visual as well as auditory images, of psychical distancing as well as direct involvement, of avant-garde as well as epic-realist techniques. The play is a complex metaphor which demonstrates Adamov's consistent vision of the "social" failure of modern man to relate to his fellow travelers as directly resulting from the absence of an interior, unifying spiritual dimension. The void without is a direct result of the void within.

---

[49] Si l'été revenait, p. 61.

CONCLUSION

Beckett has won the Nobel Prize. Ionesco is a member of the French Academy. And Adamov is dead by suicide. What we called the "theater of the absurd" in the 1950's and 1960's is to all intents and purposes over, an event in history, one of the most exciting periods in recent theater. Yet, in a very real sense, we are still so close to it in time and spirit that it is extremely difficult to evaluate it objectively.

Undoubtedly Beckett has given us the single, most important play of the generation, *En attendant Godot*. His work has been unique, exhibiting a remarkable consistency in its ceaseless variations on a single theme. His theater is primarily a theater of quest. Man is seen in search of himself. It is a "religious" theater in which man is absurdly awaiting the arrival of a god who has already passed through unnoticed. But from play to play the universe of Beckett's vision has narrowed, has become more and more bleak and ironic. It is a theater which by its very definition permits of no exit.

Ionesco was, and still is the chief spokesman for the avant-garde. It is his name that the general public most readily identifies with the experimentations and innovations of the "new theater." In contrast to Beckett, Ionesco's theater has slowly opened out from the narrow universe of the early, stylized comic-tragic parodies towards a more recognizable and "human" universe of self-analysis. And yet the theater of Ionesco remains essentially a composite image of a world whose very structure is a lie. It is a world where everything is equally valid and therefore invalid, where existence itself is unjustified, an unexplained and absurd joke.

Adamov's theater, on the other hand, is primarily a theater of statement, a concrete metaphor of a universe of absence. Man is seen as having no criteria whereby to define himself. It is a "spiritual" theater, testifying to the degradation and agony of a life which has lost the unifying spiritual dimension that man once was capable of perceiving in reality. But unlike the theater of Ionesco which posits the absurdity of the human condition as the ultimate truth of man's existence, the theater of Adamov portrays for us a world which is not absurd in itself, but rather results from man's inability to "pray," his loss of faith. Suffering and the loss of identity stem originally from "mutilation," a separation from what used to be called God, but for which today there is no name. Adamov's world of the imagination depicts the agonizing search of man, both alone and in society, for universal harmony, a wholeness, an authenticity that seems to elude him. Each man's individual search intensifies and compounds Man's search to fill the void. It is an ambitious theater whose remarkable designs and consistency deserve the success that André Pieyre de Mandiargues suggests when he called Adamov,

> . . . cet admirable personnage humain auquel nous devons une œuvre théâtrale qui n'eut pas le succès qu'elle mérite mais qui est parmi les plus remarquables de notre temps. [1]

Adamov's theater is remarkable, among other reasons, because it is a theater to be seen, a "pure" or "total" theater. His vision of the world is essentially dramatic, his metaphors and images essentially theatrical. As Leonard Pronko points out in *Avant-Garde: The Experimental Theater in France,* Adamov sees the play as a combination of text and production.

> Stressing the visible resources of the stage, he (Adamov) reminds us that drama is more than literature and that a play is only a play when it is presented on the boards before spectators. [2]

Adamov shaped a new "language of theater," a visual, even tactile language whose concerns were primarily theatrical as Beckett's were "poetic" and Ionesco's "linguistic." Beckett began with poetry, con-

---

[1] Andre Pieyré de Mandiargues, "Une Vieréussie," *Novel Observateur,* (2 juillet 1968), p. 3.

[2] Leonard Cabell Pronko, *Avant-Garde: The Experimental Theater in France,* (Berkeley and Los Angeles, 1964), p. 139.

tinued in the novel, and evolved into the theater. Ionesco began with "dialogue," a parody of the language used in foreign language text-books. Adamov began with the view of a blind beggar jostled by two young girls singing, "J'ai fermé les yeux, c'était merveilleux . . ." [3] It is this point of departure which orients Adamov's theater toward its "total" theatrical effect, a visual as well as auditory experience. More than Beckett or Ionesco, more than the "poetic" avant-garde of Vauthier, Tardieu and Pichette, Adamov wrote for the theater. He was above all else a playwright, conscious of the stage as a space to be filled with "visible" meaning.

Adamov created a theater whose "language" reflects by its patterns of audio-visual images the complexity of the human condition, the precariousness and mysteriousness of a universe where to be alone is to share a common fate, where to seek union is to realize man's inability to communicate and share. It is a special theatrical language which takes into account all aspects of life — what Marc Rombaut calls a "total" theater in the tradition of Artaud.

> Cette conception du théâtre (Adamov's) répond aux néces-
> sités d'un théâtre reflétant tous les aspects du réel. Théâtre
> total qui cherche à saisir la globalité de la vie et à la mon-
> trer ensuite dans son infinie complexité. [4]

Adamov's theater is a "total" theater not only in its formal and technical considerations, but also in its attempt to fuse thematically the existential and socio-political dilemmas of the human situation. It is a synthesis of the insoluble inner anguish of man (le mal incurable) and his more or less resolvable predicament as a victim of society and its systems (le mal curable). As the accent shifts in varying degrees within Adamov's work from the seemingly inescapable anguish of the natural law to the historical and more apparently remediable suffering of man, it becomes more and more apparent that the two levels of damnation are intimately interwoven. The particular, domestic and metaphysical hell of the human condition shares in, reflects and precedes in time the general, global political hell of the social predicament. It is this fusion of concerns which makes Adamov's

---

[3] Arthur Adamov, *Note préliminaire* in *Théâtre II*, (Paris, 1955), p. 8.

[4] Marc Rombaut, "Arthur Adamov 1908-1970," *French Review*, No. 45 (Jan. 1971), p. 6.

theater unique in contemporary French theater. Its originality lies in its freedom to follow its own natural inclination, or as Bernard Dort suggests, in its choice not to limit itself to any one known model.

> La dramaturgie adamovienne ne s'aligne sur aucune figure reconnue: ni celle du jeu circulaire pirandellien, ni celle linéaire des personnages brechtiens. [5]

By freeing itself from self-imposed limitations, by fusing "absurdist" and epic-realist statements, Adamov's theater suggests a new direction for contemporary playwrights. At the same time his symbiosis of external and subjective realism intimates a possible resolution of the age-old attempt of the theater to discover a viable means of depicting the complexity of reality.

Adamov's slow and painful elaboration of this synthesis of apparently contradictory designs has been his most original and significant contribution to modern French theater. And yet this very achievement has been misunderstood and misjudged by those who sought to fit Adamov's plays into pre-established categories. As Marc Rombaut suggests, the "rupture" or "conversion" never took place because it was never necessary.

> On a parlé de "rupture" dans l'itinéraire d'Adamov. Au dramaturge de l'avant-garde, on opposa l'auteur engagé. La rupture n'eut jamais lieu, parce que simplement son théâtre, dans son ensemble, n'a jamais répondu aux définitions d'absurde et de politique dans lesquelles on a voulu l'enfermer absolument. Adamov, et c'est une position inverse, s'est toujours proclamé partisan d'un théâtre "ouvert" et "orienté." [6]

Rather than "conversion" from one mode to another, Adamov's theater exhibits a profound unity structured on an evolving worldview which progressively discovered the interdependence of man's existential and social predicaments and presented it as such to its audience. Rather than reject the "theater of the absurd" in favor of epic-realism, Adamov's theater includes and absorbs its origins, going beyond them without actually repudiating them. It is a theater of

---

[5] Bernard Dort, "Le Théâtre d'Adamov: une scandaleuse unité," *Théâtre Magazine*, No. 1 (mars, 1969), p. 3.

[6] Rombaut, p. 6.

growth and enrichment, a total theater open to experimentation and discovery. But, as Marc Rombaut points out, most of all it is a consistent and unified theater.

> Si les conceptions théâtrales d'Adamov ont évolué depuis ses premières pièces et paraissent parfois fort éloignées de sa position au temps de sa mort, l'œuvre d'Adamov présente bien, pour reprendre cette expression paradoxale de Dort, "une scandaleuse unité." [7]

Beneath the apparent dissimilarities of content from play to play and sustaining the basic thrust of Adamov's vision of a world of absence is the repetitive or circular structure of intensification that is the unifying formal principle of his theater. Each play depicts the gradual and then rapid disintegration of its universe by the intensification by repetition of the prevailing "absence" or inauthenticity. Thus the apparent dichotomy of Adamov's theater is not a real dichotomy, but a shift in emphasis and terms, in degrees and tones. And while certain aspects tend to dominate more in one period than in another, they are consistently intermingled and interdependent throughout his entire work. Each play is in its own right just one more poetic concretization in theatrical form of the nightmares, obsessions and fears of a single, consistent vision.

---

[7] Rombaut, p. 7.

Appendix I

WORKS OF ADAMOV: IN ORDER OF COMPOSITION

Plays

La Parodie	1947
L'Invasion	1949
La grande et la petite manœuvre	1950
Le Professeur Taranne	1951
Le Sens de la Marche	1951
Tous contre tous	1952
Comme nous avons été	1953
Les Retrouvailles	1953
Le Ping-Pong	1955
Paolo Paoli	1956
Intimité	1958
La Complainte du Ridicule	1958
Je ne suis pas Français	1959
Les Ames mortes	1960
Le Printemps 71	1961
La Politique des Restes	1962
Sainte Europe	1966
M. le Modéré	1967
Off Limits	1968
Si l'été revenait	1970

Translations

Georg Büchner. *La Mort de Danton*	1948
Maxime Gorki. *Les petits bourgeois*	1959

Other Writings

L'Aveu	1938-43
Auguste Strindberg, Dramaturge	1955
Ici et maintenant	1950-63
L'Homme et L'Enfant	1967-68
Je....ils	1969

PLAYS OF ADAMOV: IN ORDER OF FIRST PERFORMANCE

La grande et la petite manœuvre. November 11, 1950, Théâtre des Noctambules, directed by Jean-Marie Serreau.

L'Invasion. November 14, 1950, Studio des Champs Elysées, directed by Jean Vilar.

La Parodie. June 5, 1952, Théâtre Lancry, directed by Roger Blin.

Le Professeur Taranne. March 18, 1953, Théâtre de la Comédie, directed by Roger Planchon.

Le Sens de la marche. March 18, 1953, Théâtre de la Comédie, directed by Roger Planchon.

Tous contre tous. April 14, 1953, Théâtre de l'Œuvre, directed by Jean-Marie Serreau.

Comme nous avons été. March 21, 1954, Théâtre de l'Œuvre, directed by Jacques Mauclair.

Le Ping-Pong. March 2, 1955, Théâtre des Noctambules, directed by Jacques Mauclair.

Paolo Paoli. May 24, 1957, Théâtre de la Comédie, directed by Roger Planchon.

Les Ames mortes. April 16, 1960, Théâtre de France, directed by Roger Planchon.

Le Printemps 71. April 26, 1963, Théâtre Gérard-Philipe, directed by Claude Martin.

La Politique des restes. May 31, 1963, Unity Theatre, directed by Gabriel Garran.

M. le Modéré. April 12, 1968, Théâtre des Mathurins, directed by Gabriel Garran.

Off Limits. January 24, 1969, Théâtre de la Commune d'Auber-
villiers, directed by Gabriel Garran.

Plays listed below, to my knowledge, have not yet been produced.

Les Retrouvailles
Intimité
La Complainte du ridicule
Je ne suis pas Français
Sainte Europe
Si l'été revenait

BIBLIOGRAPHY

I

Adamov, Arthur: *Les Ames mortes*, Paris: Gallimard, 1960.
———: *Auguste Strindberg, Dramaturge*, Paris: L'Arche, 1955.
———: *L'Aveu*, Paris: Editions du Sagittaire, 1946.
———: *Comme nous avons été*, La Nouvelle Nouvelle Revue Française, 1: 3, 1953.
———: *L'Homme et L'Enfant*, Paris: Gallimard, 1968.
———: *Ici et maintenant*, Paris: Gallimard, 1964.
———: *Je.... ils....*, Paris: Gallimard, 1969.
———: *Off Limits*, Paris: Gallimard, 1969.
———: *Paolo Paoli*, Paris: Gallimard, 1957.
———: *La Parodie, L'Invasion*, précédées d'une lettre d'André Gide, et des témoignages de René Char, Jacques Prévert, Henri Thomas, Jacques Lemarchand, Jean Vilar, Roger Blin. Paris: Charlot, 1950.
———: *Le Printemps 71*, Paris: Gallimard, 1961.
———: *Si l'été revenait*, Paris: Gallimard, 1970.
———: *Théâtre I*, Paris: Gallimard, 1953.
———: *Théâtre II*, Paris: Gallimard, 1955.
———: *Théâtre III*, Paris: Gallimard, 1966.
———: *Théâtre IV*, Paris: Gallimard, 1968.
———: *Théâtre de Société*, Paris: Les Editeurs Français Réunis, 1958.

II

Apollinaire, Guillaume: *Les Mamelles de Tirésais*, Paris: Gallimard, 1946.
Artaud, Antonin: *Le Théâtre et son double*, Paris: Gallimard, 1964.
Barthes, Roland: *Essais critiques*, Paris: Editions du Seuil, 1964.
———: *Mythologies*, Paris: Editions du Seuil, 1957.
Béhar, Henri: *Etude sur le théâtre dada et surréaliste*, Paris: Gallimard, 1967.
Beigbeder, Marc: *Le Théâtre en France depuis la libération*, Paris: Bordas, 1959.
Champigny, Robert: *Le Genre dramatique*, Monte-Carlo: Editions Regain, 1965.
Dort, Bernard: Les pièces d'Adamov, *Les Temps modernes*, 6: 63, 1951.

Dort, Bernard: Le Théâtre d'Adamov: une scandaleuse unité, *Théâtre Magazine*, 1: 1, 1969.

Duvignaud, Jean: *Sociologie du Théâtre*, Paris: Presses Universitaires De France, 1965.

————: Le Théâtre d'Adamov, *La Nouvelle Nouvelle Revue Française*, 2: 22, 1954.

————: Le Théâtre de promesse, *La Nouvelle Nouvelle Revue Française*, 1: 3, 1953.

Esslin, Martin: *The Theatre of the Absurd*, New York: Doubleday and Company, 1961.

Goldmann, Lucien: *Jean Racine, Dramaturge*, Paris: L'Arche, 1956.

Gouhier, Henri: *Le Théâtre et L'Existence*, Paris: Editions Montaigne, 1952.

Grossvogel, David I.: *20th Century Drama*, New York: Columbia University Press, 1961.

Guicharnaud, Jacques, in collaboration with June Guicharnaud: *Modern French Theatre from Giraudoux to Genet*. Revised ed. New Haven and London: Yale University Press, 1967.

Lemarchand, Jacques: *M. le Modéré* d'Arthur Adamov, *Le Figaro littéraire*, 7: 13, 1968.

Lynes, Jr., Carlos: Adamov or "le sens littéral" in the Theater, *Yale French Studies*, 14: 1, 1954-55.

Mandiargues, André Pieyre de: Une Vie réussie, *Nouvel Observateur*, 2 juillet, 1968.

Poirot-Delpech, B.: *Off Limits* d'Arthur Adamov, *Le Monde*, 22: 6, 1969.

Pronko, Leonard Cabell: *Avant-Garde: The Experimental Theater in France*, Berkeley and Los Angeles: University of California Press, 1962.

Ransom, John Crowe: *The New Criticism*, Norfolk: New Directions, 1941.

Rombaut, Marc: Arthur Adamov 1908-1970, *French Review*, 45: 1, 1971.

Saurel, Renée: *Tous contre tous* d'Arthur Adamov, *Les Temps modernes*, 8: 91, 1953.

Serreau, Geneviève: *Histoire du "nouveau théâtre"*, Paris: Gallimard, 1966.

Sherrell, Richard E.: Arthur Adamov and Invaded Man, *Modern Drama 7*, 7: 2, 1965.

Wellwarth, George E.: *The Theater of Protest and Paradox*, New York: New York University Press, 1964.

————: Alfred Jarry: The Seed of the Avant-Garde Drama, *Criticism*, 4: 1, 1962.

Zand, Nicole: Entretien avec Arthur Adamov, *Le Monde*, 22: 1, 1969.

INDEX OF AUTHORS QUOTED

INDEX OF MAJOR THEMES